THE BELIEVER'S SECURITY:

CONDITIONAL or UNCONDITIONAL?

(ADDRESSING FALSE DOCTRINE IN THE CHURCH)

by

DANIEL D. CORNER

Unless otherwise noted, Scripture quotations are from the New International Version of the Bible.

ISBN No. 0-9639076-5-4

Additional copies of this book may be obtained by making your check or money order payable to:

Evangelical Outreach
P. O. Box 265
Washington, PA 15301-0265

(See page 110 for prices.)

Printed in the United States of America
by Reed & Witting Co. of Pittsburgh, PA.

"FOR OF THIS YOU CAN BE SURE: **No immoral, impure or greedy person** - such a man is an idolater - **has any inheritance in the kingdom of Christ and of God. LET NO ONE DECEIVE YOU WITH EMPTY WORDS,** for because of such things God's wrath comes on those who are disobedient. Therefore do not be partners with them" (Eph. 5:5-7).

"But whoever disowns me before men, **I will DISOWN him before my Father in heaven**" (Matt. 10:33).

"Anyone who runs ahead and **does not continue** in the teaching of Christ **DOES NOT HAVE GOD; whoever continues in the teaching has both the Father and the Son**" (2 Jn. 9).

"By this gospel you are saved, **IF** you hold firmly to the word I preached to you. **Otherwise, you have BELIEVED IN VAIN**" (1 Cor. 15:2).

"But now he has reconciled you by Christ's physical body through death to present you holy in his sight, without blemish and free from accusation - **IF YOU CONTINUE IN YOUR FAITH, established and firm, not moved from the hope held out in the gospel. THIS IS THE GOSPEL THAT YOU HEARD** and that has been proclaimed to every creature under heaven..." (Col. 1:22,23).

"We have come to share in Christ **IF we hold firmly TILL THE END the confidence we had at first**" (Heb. 3:14).

Word of Acknowledgement

With sincere gratitude, I would like to thank Jane Ivanhoe, Toni Ivanhoe, Mike Aiello, Jim Aiello and his wife, Debbie, for their time spent proofing this work. Their suggestions have helped to improve the quality of this study.

After the Lord, I would like to thank my beloved wife, Cheryl, the most for her excellent suggestions regarding grammar and doctrine. Her untold long hours laboring with me in the formation of this book can only be fully appreciated by her Lord and her husband. Without her this book would have been an impossibility.

Thank you, Lord, for the privilege You have given me in writing this book. May You be pleased to use it in whatever capacity You may so desire.

Contents

* Introduction *

This book began as a tract on this subject! After getting started, however, there were so many important points not made and questions not dealt with that it grew and grew into a book. Please know that it is still not an exhaustive work on this subject. It does, however, from a Scriptural point of view, cite many sound objections to the teaching of unconditional eternal security in both offensive and defensive ways.

In this book you'll notice names of popular teachers. To name names was often done by Paul and others in both a favorable way (Phil. 2:22; 2 Tim. 1:16-18) and an unfavorable way (Phil. 4:2; Col. 4:17; 2 Tim. 2:17,18; 4:14,15; 3 Jn. 9,10; etc.). Therefore, don't think this is, in itself, unscriptural. In fact, it is advantageous to clearly know who is teaching what!

Moreover, don't be deceived about the meaning of "touch not God's anointed" (K.J.V.) as used by many to mean: don't adversely speak out against a Bible teacher's doctrine or actions. This phrase, which is commonly misused, refers to PHYSICAL HARM, that is, don't physically hurt one of God's anointed. While David "touched not God's anointed" (1 Sam. 24:10), he verbally corrected him (Saul) before his army (1 Sam. 26:7-25)! Also, all Christians are anointed, not just the teachers (1 Jn. 2:20)! Finally, Paul openly rebuked the Apostle Peter before others, then wrote of it in one of his epistles for truth's sake (Gal. 2:11-13).

Furthermore, the cited teachers do have many excellent teachings, even though they embrace the Calvinistic doctrine of unconditional eternal security (U. E. S.). So do not judge the merit of this work by their sound teachings and advice in other areas. They are often right, which unfortunately, makes U. E. S. more believable to their audience. (It's possible to have excellent teachings in many areas with a horrible teaching attached! A prime example of this is Ron Rhodes' book, Reasoning From The Scriptures With The Jehovah's Witnesses. This excellent refutation to the many heresies of Jehovah's Witnesses, unfortunately, has the error of U. E. S. mixed in it too![1] Many other books and cassette tapes on apologetics and countering cults include the myth of U. E. S. How grieving to read or hear such, especially when the primary message is given to correct error, and for the most part, does an excellent job!)

This book, therefore, primarily deals with false teaching within the church. However, this same teaching seems to be a favorite among the unrepentant who don't gather with the saints any more!

In light of this, just before this book was printed, one professing Christian and unconditional eternal security proponent **unashamedly** admitted to this author that he was sexually immoral! This man displayed no apparent fear of Hell or even of God's painful discipline, but wanted to defend his doctrinal position!

I distinctly remember a different U. E. S. adherent who was profane, an occasional drunkard and, by his own admittance, sexually immoral. Yet, he clung tenaciously to his profession that he was, indeed, a Christian based on U. E. S.! (He also hadn't been to church for years.) **When I offered several Scriptural reasons why this doctrine is false, he got angry and didn't want to hear any more.**

A particular U. E. S. pastor/teacher, before his Sunday School class, declared his view of Scripture as being *an adulterer might still go to Heaven,* based on this teaching. He kept insisting that only God knows the heart and he was unable to judge whether such a man was saved or not! Could it be that this pastor doesn't know a judgment of one's heart is not involved, since the Bible clearly speaks out against this behavior (1 Cor. 6:9,10; Gal. 5:19-21; etc.)?

Yet another U. E. S. advocate told me that someone can be "*completely backslidden*" and still be saved! With emotion in his voice he endeavored to cite Scriptural proof for his statement regarding the sexually immoral! Furthermore, the first thing out of this particular man's mouth after I stated the Bible does not teach U. E. S. was that my position is "*a work's salvation*"! My answer was, **"Paul, the grace teacher, didn't believe in it. How, then, could it be a work's salvation?"** (Scriptural proof for this is cited in the main part of this study.)

How could controversy exist over the sexually immoral when Paul, the grace teacher, clearly said numerous times such won't enter the kingdom of heaven?

What would an unbeliever think about such people as these U. E. S. proponents? Do you think this type of talk has caused confusion about the type of lifestyle a Christian is to be living?

Also, the "assurance of salvation" message has a place in Scripture, but it's not the kind of Scriptural teaching that ignores unrepented and unconfessed sin in the believer's life. Such people, in rebellion to God, are being dealt with by the **Holy**

Spirit to REPENT. **IT IS NOT THE DEVIL**, as the U. E. S. teachers would say, who is making them unassured in their spiritual stand before God!

Moreover, the beloved U. E. S. teaching destroys the **healthy fear** that Paul commanded the Christians at Rome to have about their spiritual status (Rom. 11:20).

What shocking nonsense exists under the banner of sound doctrine - and much because of this popular teaching. Whatever happened to holy and righteous living? It seems that some are trying to justify, with Scripture, unholy living and disobedience. Let 1 Thess. 4:7,8 make an indelible impression on your heart: **"For God did not call us to be impure, but to live a holy life. Therefore, he who rejects this instruction does not reject man but God, who gives you his Holy Spirit."**

Dear reader, what you accept as truth **will** influence your behavior. For example, if you accepted the lie that the Watchtower Society is Jehovah's Organization, you would be attending a Kingdom Hall somewhere! Similarly, to accept U. E. S. as truth will behaviorally affect you, to some degree. This reminds me of a growing, zealous Christian, who was doing fine for about nine months after his salvation, until he accepted U. E. S. as truth. He then immediately backslid spiritually, became very worldly and lost his evangelistic zeal! Not all U. E. S. proponents suffer spiritually like this, but many besides the one cited certainly have!

It has also been my observation that those who believe in U. E. S. are living in a false security like the people who were on board the Titanic in April of 1912 thinking it was impossible for them to go down in the ship. **They rested in a security they firmly believed in, but which didn't really exist!** As a consequence, the majority died needlessly, because there wasn't an adequate number of lifeboats! The people would have been much better off to know the disturbing truth that a real danger did presently exist even for them! To deny the danger, though somewhat comforting, doesn't make it disappear! It only makes such people easier prey. This ministry doesn't want YOU or YOUR FAMILY or YOUR FRIENDS to be the devil's prey! That's why this book has been written, though it's certain that adverse criticism will come to this author.

This book is not a defense of Jacob Arminius or his teachings, but a presentation and defense of the teachings of the Lord Jesus and His apostles on the subject of the believer's security.

1

✻ What is Unconditional Eternal Security? ✻

The days that we are living in are certainly "terrible" ones (2 Tim. 3:1). The rampant, growing wickedness worldwide among the unsaved is, however, only part of the problem.

Unfortunately, even in the church there are serious doctrinal problems that add to the perils of our day, sometimes to the point of affecting one's behavior, that is, in holy or unholy living, and thereby affecting eternal destinies! Let's examine one of these areas which has been a continuing controversy among the redeemed for centuries - the believer's security, also known by other names such as the perseverance of the saints, **unconditional eternal security** or just plain **eternal security.**

This is a very important truth to grasp, for it will certainly shade one's understanding of the entire Bible. Is it true, as many say: "Once saved, **ALWAYS** saved" or "Once in grace, **ALWAYS** in grace"? The other side of this controversy states that a real, Bible-defined Christian **MUST** "endure **to the end** to be saved" (Matt. 10:22) and **MUST** "hold firmly **till the end** to share in Christ" (Heb. 3:14).

The doctrine of unconditional eternal security (U. E. S.) has two strands: (1) The ***extreme view*** states if one was truly saved, then falls into drunkenness, sexual immorality, greed, etc., he/she is still saved and can never perish; (2) The ***moderate view*** would say that same person was never really saved at all, since his present sins contradict his profession of faith. Or, as one U. E. S. teacher, Jack Van Impe, wrote: "*We see, then, that it **is** possible for any child of God to commit sin but **impossible** for the genuine believer to live a **life** of sin*"[2] (emphasis his).

Seemingly, the majority of the Christian authors and teachers on TV and radio hold to the doctrine of U. E. S. for the believer in Christ. "Certainly," some must be thinking, "there are very learned men among their ranks who have thoroughly examined both sides of this controversy and have accurately come to their current conclusion." Or, is it possible they have come to a wrong conclusion for whatever reason? Are they really accurately representing the opposing position, giving the best reasons Scripturally why certain Christians hold to the other view? Is it right for them to scream "bondage" or "legalism" when someone opposes their view? [There is obviously something seriously wrong with the present-day grace message which equates obedience with legalism!]

Please remember the popularity of a teacher or the number of renowned "scholars" who hold to a particular position does not, in itself, make it correct. **It is only the weight of Scripture that should drive us to a certain doctrinal view, 2 Tim. 3:16,17.** Also, the desire to believe a doctrine should not even be a consideration in our doctrinal decisions.

Is it true that if one holds to the view that a Christian can possibly "fall away" and end up in Hell, HE IS BELIEVING THAT HIS OWN GOOD WORKS WILL SAVE HIM OR KEEP HIM SAVED, as the U. E. S. teachers would usually accuse? Or, is this accusation itself **FALSE** and **MISLEADING, MISREPRESENTING** the opposing side in an effort to immediately **DISCREDIT** it? What did Paul, the **great grace teacher**, say regarding this? Some readers may be quite surprised as the evidence is cited a little later!

[Please remember that one is a Christian on the basis of being Biblically "born again" alone. His doctrines about certain things do not have to be 100% accurate. In other words, there are true Christians on both sides of this controversy.]

Many sincere proponents of the U. E. S. doctrine feel it is basic to Christianity and therefore often immediately teach it to the newly saved. Some have even gone so far as to teach it along with the salvation message to the unsaved, as perhaps you have observed from certain salvation tracts! Still other U. E. S. adherents seem to gauge the worth of a Christian ministry on this doctrine alone! In other words, they claim that a ministry isn't really "sound" and should be avoided if it's not taught!

Notice how prevalent this teaching is! The late John R. Rice, another U. E. S. teacher, wrote:

> *"It is vitally important to have a clear understanding of this most basic and fundamental doctrine of 'ETERNAL SALVATION.' The truth is, if you don't understand the 'ETERNAL SECURITY ' of God's people you do NOT understand what it means to 'BELIEVE ON CHRIST!'* "[3] (emphasis his).

Similarly, in his book on the marks of cults, Dave Breese, a different U. E. S. author, includes a chapter entitled, "Uncertain Hope." In it he said:

> "*We may be very sure that the promoter of a false religion who is interested in promoting dependence upon himself as against freedom that comes through faith in Christ would never pass on to his followers the words of Christ, 'My sheep hear My voice, and I know them, and they follow Me; And I give unto them eternal life;* ***and they shall never perish****, neither shall any man pluck them out of My hand. My Father, which gave them Me, is greater than all; and no man is able to pluck them out of My Father's hand' (John 10:27-29). It is interesting to note that the verse immediately following this promise says, 'Then the Jews took up stones again to stone Him.' Natural men, even in the realm of religious leadership, will do anything to destroy the perfect confidence that a relationship with Jesus Christ brings to a life. The reason is very clear,* ***they traffic in anxiety***" [4] (emphasis his, but bold here is italics in original).

[Please note the blatant error just stated by this popular TV teacher and author, that is, the Jews wanted to stone Jesus in Jn. 10:30 because they didn't like His message on "the perfect confidence that a relationship with Jesus Christ brings to a life." **The truth is: they wanted to stone Him because they wrongly thought He was guilty of blasphemy, for He claimed to be God**, v.33! Furthermore, to imply it is cultic to not believe in U. E. S. <u>or</u> it is contrary to "freedom that comes through faith in Christ" is WRONG! Regarding Christian freedom, remember: **the true "freedom that comes through faith in Christ" message will never conflict with righteous and godly living!**]

In contrast to these authors, many other Christians view U. E. S. as one of the best doctrines the devil has ever used to infiltrate the church! Such believe this teaching has adversely affected the behavior of multiple millions - indirectly sending many of them to Hell and creating a general, dangerous laxness among others who have accepted it!

If this teaching is wrong, it would have to be under the category of "**ear tickling**" and not a "*glorious truth*" as some call it! Also, we who know the truth should openly speak out and refute it in Christian love, for the sake of the eternal souls that can yet be reached.

2

✻ The Dangerous Trio ✻

The Scriptures reveal that **CERTAIN SINS, FALSE DOCTRINE ABOUT SALVATION, and PERSECUTION** all hold within their potential the possibility of negating one's salvation, or, to put it in Jesus' words, one can "**lose** his own soul" (Mk. 8:36, K.J.V.). [You can't **lose** what you had secured in a bank unless you really had something there to begin with; neither can you "**lose**" your soul if it wasn't first saved!]

If you're a U. E. S. proponent, before you reject this as a possibility, please closely consider the following Scripturally-based arguments. Don't let the traditions of men or wishful thinking hold you in a **dangerous deception** regarding your present Christian race! Let only the weight of Scripture sway you, and not emotional ties to your parents, natural or spiritual, and/or brothers or sisters in Christ!

I. SOUL-DAMNING SINS

All sins are not the same in their effect on our souls. Some sins are "greater" than other sins (Jn. 19:11). One type of sin is "eternal" (Mk. 3:29), while others are not. Another type of sin is uniquely "against" our own bodies, while other sins are "outside" our bodies (1 Cor. 6:18). Finally, 1 Jn. 5:16 declares that there is "a sin that does NOT lead to death," while there is "a sin that leads to death." Now let's proceed regarding the most serious types of sins, the soul-damning ones.

After Paul listed the acts of the sinful nature: "sexual immorality, impurity and debauchery; idolatry and witchcraft; hatred, discord, jealousy, fits of rage, selfish ambition, dissensions, factions and envy; drunkenness, orgies, and the like" (Gal. 5:19-21), he then said, "...**I**

WARN <u>**YOU**</u>, as I did before, that those who live like this **WILL NOT INHERIT THE KINGDOM OF GOD**" (v. 21). This, therefore, was **a valid "warning" that he REPEATEDLY ISSUED directly to real Christians for they themselves to take to heart! [PLEASE**

PAUL'S REPEATED WARNING DIRECTED TO CHRISTIANS ABOUT THE SINFUL NATURE

NOTE, ACCORDING TO THIS, YOUR DOCTRINE CAN BE 100% SOUND IN EVERY AREA, YET YOU <u>**WILL**</u> **STILL GO TO HELL IF YOUR SINFUL NATURE IS IN CONTROL OF YOUR LIFE!]**

Notice the clear evidence that the Galatians were indeed Christians: Paul preached the gospel to them (4:13), they accepted it (1:9), became his spiritual children (4:19), and were running a good spiritual race (5:7) before false teachers came along and threw them into confusion (5:10). Even more clear is Gal. 3:2, which shows in question form that **they received the Holy Spirit** by their belief (or faith), which would be impossible for the unsaved. Undoubtedly then, **Paul issued this MOST SEVERE "warning" MULTIPLE TIMES to real Christians, because it was still possible for them to miss Heaven!** If this Holy Spirit inspired warning was not heeded - then the acts of the sinful nature in these Christians' lives would cause them "NOT to inherit the kingdom of God"! Notice that **Paul did NOT say they would merely miss out on eternal rewards, treasures and/or crowns, as some would say!** Neither did he merely say their "fellowship" with God would be adversely affected! Instead, he said **they, who were Christians at the moment, WOULD DEFINITELY miss Heaven altogether! Why? Because of certain SINS, as he cited.**

Another U. E. S. teacher, David Levy, wrote the following about this passage:

> *"The apostle included the sober warning that those 'who do such things [i.e., habitually practice these sins] shall not inherit the kingdom of God' (v.21). He was not saying that Christians can lose their salvation by committing any of these sins mentioned but that the habitual practice of such sins would indicate that the people committing them are not saved."* [5]

Please note the following: (1) Levy is right in saying it is a habitual practice of sin in this passage, as the Greek shows. However, other similar passages condemn certain people (identified by their prevailing sin) long before it's a habitual practice! One example found in Scripture is in Lev. 20:10, "If a man commits adultery with another man's wife - with the wife of his neighbor - both the adulterer and adulteress must be put to death." Though we don't carry out this punishment in our day, we nonetheless can learn from this Scripture. It only takes one act to commit adultery and thereby be Scripturally labeled an "adulterer" or "adulteress," which means one will NOT (even if once saved) inherit the kingdom of God, according to 1 Cor. 6:9,10, that is, unless he/she repents! If one act of adultery does NOT make a person an "adulterer" or "adulteress," then how many acts does it take - two, five, twenty, fifty? Can you back your answer up with Scripture? How many times does a person have to murder to be a murderer? (2) To attribute Levy's interpretation to this passage: *"He [Paul] was not saying that Christians can lose their salvation by committing any of the sins mentioned but that the habitual practice of such would indicate that the people committing them are not saved"* is to be blind to the clear and obvious! Certainly, those that habitually practice the sins cited are NOT saved, but **this isn't the point Paul was making to the Galatian Christians!** Instead, he was speaking directly to them and **WARNING** them, as he had done previously, of A REAL DANGER which still EXISTED EVEN THOUGH THEY WERE ALREADY CHRISTIANS AND WHICH IS CLEARLY IDENTIFIED AS MISSING THE KINGDOM OF GOD!

In the natural, if a loving family member would WARN his relatives by letter that they should NOT build their home in the low lands near a particular river, because of a long history of annual, devastating flooding, **should we understand that he meant this WARNING only for a different person or group of people, such as those already in the low lands by that river?** What would you personally think of such a person's ability to read? Furthermore, isn't it implied in the word "**warning**" that a very real DANGER exists even for the relatives, that is, if the one who issued the warning is informed? In this case, the danger would be losing his home and belongings therein contained. (In the case of the Scriptural passage, the danger for the Christian is missing the kingdom of God.) (3) To be forewarned of danger, though disturbing, is beneficial or **advantageous!** To know that you're in rattlesnake country before a hike into the woods is beneficial over the absence of this knowledge. Conversely, the benefit of this type of Pauline WARNING issued to the Galatian Christians is not only missing, but clearly denied by the U. E. S. teachers, as Levy demonstrates. Therefore, spiritual harm, to some undetermined degree, occurs to those who listen to and accept U. E. S. as Biblical fact. Advocates of U. E. S., therefore, are at a disadvantage just like in the natural if a warning is omitted or explained away! The disadvantage is proportionate to the danger, which in this case, is **the ultimate danger of eternal suffering in fire!**

A corroborating verse to Gal. 5:19-21 is Rom. 8:13 which reads, **"FOR IF YOU LIVE ACCORDING TO THE SINFUL NATURE, YOU WILL DIE; BUT IF BY THE SPIRIT YOU PUT TO DEATH THE MISDEEDS OF THE BODY, YOU WILL LIVE."** Please note that the "death" promised to Christians who decide to live according to the sinful nature has to be SPIRITUAL death, and not physical death, since **ONLY those who "live according to the sinful nature" will experience this death.** Please note, according to Jesus, when the Prodigal Son decided to live according to the sinful nature, he did NOT "die" physically, but did **"DIE" SPIRITUALLY** (Lk. 15:24,32)! Again, the true grace teacher, Paul, in Rom. 8:13 reveals a side of grace that far too many in our day are not aware of and would never want to understand! Also, **notice how DEFINITE spiritual death will be**, if one chooses to "live according to the sinful nature" (Rom. 8:13). **Unlike what some are teaching, Paul taught that even after the Savior's death, SIN IS STILL AN ISSUE WITH GOD!**

Paul also wrote: "...A man reaps what he sows. The one who sows to please his sinful nature, from that nature **WILL REAP DESTRUCTION;** the one who sows to please the Spirit, from the Spirit **will reap eternal life**" (Gal. 6:7,8). Though you probably heard

SOW TO PLEASE THE SINFUL NATURE AND REAP DESTRUCTION AS OPPOSED TO ETERNAL LIFE.

these sowing and reaping verses used many other ways, in context they refer only to sowing to please the sinful nature or to please the Spirit! See also **Rom. 6:16 cf. vv. 21,22.**

Hal Lindsey, another popular U. E. S. teacher, would declare this as being *"jerked out of context,"* while he offers a ridiculous interpretation as the correct one! He wrote:

> *"Now some of you may be saying, 'All right, Hal, if God never punishes us for our sins, what about Galatians 6:7 which says, 'Do not be deceived, God is not mocked; for whatever a man sows, this he will also reap'? ' This verse is jerked out of context by so many Christians that*

> *it's incredible. The verse just before this one says, 'And let the one who is taught the Word share all good things with him who teaches' (Galatians 6:6). This context is talking about supporting financially the one who gives himself to studying and teaching the Bible....This concept of 'whatsoever a man sows, he shall also reap' is concerned with investing our money in God's work and the reward or lack of reward for our stewardship."* [6]

Also, remember **it was Paul, the great GRACE TEACHER himself,** who wrote Gal. 6:7,8! He also issued the warning in Gal. 5:21 which indicates not just some insignificant danger, but the **ULTIMATE ETERNAL DANGER OF GOING TO THE LAKE OF FIRE,** the only other place to go if one does "not inherit the kingdom of God" (Matt. 7:13,14; 25:34-46 and Rev. 21:1-8)!

If Paul in a disguise could stand in many so-called "evangelical churches" today and speak out the exact words of Gal. 5:21 for the first time to the Christians present, he would probably be falsely charged with implying that we keep ourselves saved by our own good works! Some might even ridiculously accuse him of not understanding "grace" or the keeping power of a loving God, or perhaps down playing the infinite work of Christ!

Finally, regarding Gal. 5:19-21, let it be stated dogmatically that **NO U. E. S. teacher could ever issue such a helpful and important WARNING OF ULTIMATE SPIRITUAL DANGER TO CHRISTIANS THAT THEY COULD STILL "NOT INHERIT THE KINGDOM OF GOD" as Paul did in these verses!** Paul, therefore, could NOT have been a U. E. S. adherent, as we know one today! In fact, there is evidence that he actually fought against this type of false doctrine, as you shall soon see! Therefore, his understanding of Scriptural GRACE must have been much different than is being presented today by many popular teachers and authors!

True grace teaching is clearly shown in Tit. 2:11,12 which says, "For the grace of God that brings salvation has appeared to all men. It teaches us to say 'No' to ungodliness and worldly passions, and to live self-controlled, upright and godly lives in this present age...." In other words, true grace teaching will promote holy living NOT IMMORALITY!

In Eph. 5:3-7, another very similar warning, as cited in Gal. 5:19-21, was given to the Christians at Ephesus. Verses 5-7 read, "**FOR OF THIS YOU CAN BE SURE:** No immoral, impure or greedy person - such a man is an idolater - **HAS ANY INHERITANCE IN THE KINGDOM OF CHRIST AND OF GOD. LET NO ONE DECEIVE**

YOU WITH EMPTY WORDS, FOR BECAUSE OF SUCH THINGS God's wrath comes on those who are disobedient. Therefore do not be partners with them."

Please note the following five observations from these three verses: (1) "God's wrath" is equated with Him **REMOVING** a Christian's inheritance in His kingdom. New Jerusalem is part of that inheritance as is the promised paradise environment with no more death, mourning, crying or pain, according to Rev. 21:1-7! (2) If one is "**immoral, impure or greedy**" he is NOT saved from eternal damnation, as his sin shows his heart condition and lack of faith **at the moment**, though he might have been truly saved in the past, still presently professes to be saved and still attends, as we say in our day, "church." Paul repeats this basic truth in 1 Cor. 6:9,10. (3) Any message contradictory to Eph. 5:3-7 is "empty" of truth, though it might be sprinkled with Biblical terminology from glib, religious teachers in influential positions. (4) Even Christians can be "deceived" by this type of empty teaching about sin's serious consequences. **[Friend, don't YOU be deceived even though some TV and radio teachers or pastors (even yours) are teaching to the contrary!]** (5) A real Christian can indeed commit these sins, hence forfeiting his spiritual inheritance.

> **PAUL'S "ASSURANCE MESSAGE":**
>
> ***"FOR OF THIS YOU CAN BE SURE: NO IMMORAL, IMPURE OR GREEDY PERSON - SUCH A MAN IS AN IDOLATER - HAS ANY INHERITANCE IN THE KINGDOM OF CHRIST AND OF GOD. LET NO ONE DECEIVE YOU WITH EMPTY WORDS..."*** **(EPH. 5:5,6).**

In regard to this entire section on sin, let me quote again the staunch U. E. S. teacher-author, John R. Rice, with his extreme position:

> *"David committed sins of murder and adultery. We must condemn his sins. They were bad. But David's*

> *sins were under the blood of Christ, and in the fifty-first Psalm, the prayer of David shows that* ***he had NOT lost his salvation, but the joy of salvation***" [7] (emphasis ours).

Beloved, as Paul wrote, "**let no one deceive you with empty words**" such as these! David, like anyone else, would **NOT** enter the kingdom of God, unless he repented of these soul-damning sins! Paul clearly stated that people who are sexually immoral will NOT inherit the kingdom of God (1 Cor. 6:9,10)! David was not an exception to this. **DO NOT BE DECEIVED!** This shows again that Paul, the true grace teacher, was NOT teaching the same as the popular, but misleading, U. E. S. teachers of our day or in the past! **Paul was also unlike many pastors and evangelists of our hour, in that he was willing to risk being misunderstood and to be labeled "divisive" over God's truth on this issue, WHICH IS VITAL, since it's indirectly related to the salvation message!** Furthermore, regarding David, Rev. 21:8 declares that no murderer will escape the lake of fire, that is, unless he/she repents! Rev. 21:8 is another reason how we KNOW FOR CERTAIN that David lost more than just the joy of his salvation over his sins of adultery and murder.

By the way, **Psalm 51 doesn't say David didn't lose his salvation!** The way some U. E. S. adherents read into Psalm 51 what they want to see is a prime example of how NOT to interpret the Bible!

The more moderate U. E. S. view regarding the David-Bathsheba-Uriah scenario would be unwittingly or indirectly stating that David was NEVER REALLY SAVED TO BEGIN WITH, since he committed sins of adultery and murder! But how can that be since, afterwards, he asked God to forgive him and RESTORE the joy of his salvation (Psalm 51)! Obviously, there is a problem here too for the moderate U. E. S. proponent, since David was clearly saved BEFORE he committed these soul-damning sins!

Jude 4 clearly states that there were people in that day "**who change the grace of our God into a license for immorality.**" (This seems to have been a common problem then, as it is today.) A perverted message under the banner of "grace" was promoting immorality instead of holy living. This is what the "contend for the faith" command is all about in Jude 3! Therefore, this perverted grace message was countered by Jude in his epistle and by Paul, as well, in Eph. 5:3-7 and elsewhere. **Teachings such as what you just read regarding David's sins allegedly not keeping him out of the kingdom of God, are giving a "license for immorality," as Jude put it!** Many people would quickly gratify the sinful desire of sexual immorality at the expense of spiritual rewards and even chastisement.

However, if such people knew the truth they would be much slower to yield to such a soul-damning sin!

As already referred to, Paul stated in his first epistle to the Corinthians (6:9,10): "Do you not know that **the wicked will NOT inherit the kingdom of God? DO NOT BE DECEIVED**: Neither the sexually immoral nor idolaters nor adulterers nor male prostitutes nor homosexual offenders nor thieves nor the greedy nor drunkards nor slanderers nor swindlers will inherit the kingdom of God." There are MANY Christians today that are "deceived" about these sins, even though we have this clear Biblical statement! **Many have been DECEIVED BY U. E. S. TEACHERS! Under their banner of "grace" such sins were and are being committed without any fear of spiritual death!**

Perhaps Charles Stanley is the most popular U. E. S. teacher on TV and radio. He said in one of his sermons:

> *"I mean the moment back there you placed your trust in Jesus Christ, my friend, from that moment on that's it - saved and secured and certain forever and all the proof is in the Word."* [8]

Immediately, a Christian should sense there is something **very wrong** with this position in the light of 1 Cor. 6:9,10; Eph. 5:3-7; Gal. 5:19-21; etc. The real grace teacher said, in contrast to many popular, present-day "grace" teachers, that people who commit the sins listed in these passages **will NOT inherit the kingdom of God**! In other words, they are soul-damning sins. This is true even though they might have been saved in the past. Why then are there so many deceived Christians believing otherwise? Could it be that they spend too much time listening to teachings and reading popular Christian books instead of **studying their own Bibles closely with an open and teachable heart, willing to yield to Scriptural findings?** Before we look more closely at other ways to "forfeit" one's soul (Mk. 8:36), let's finish dealing with the subject of **SIN**.

Rom. 8:35-39 is commonly cited in such a way by the U. E. S. teachers as to convey the meaning to be that even certain sins, **though the word "sin" is not listed**, cannot "separate" Christians from the love of Christ, thereby suggesting that God's children are unconditionally secure, regardless of their present or future sins! Cal Beisner, another U. E. S. teacher, stated:

> *"Nothing can separate the believer from the love of Christ - nothing in all creation, and God Himself will*

> *not separate the believer from Him (Romans 8:35-39, cf. vv. 32-34; John 10:27-29)*" [9] (emphasis his).

This, however, can NOT be the meaning of Rom. 8:35-39 since **SIN MOST DEFINITELY DOES "SEPARATE" FROM GOD AS ISA. 59:2 CLEARLY DECLARES.** This passage reads, "But your iniquities have **SEPARATED** you from your God; your sins have hidden his face from you, so that he will not hear." Remember, the Prodigal Son, when with the prostitutes (Lk. 15:30), was so spiritually SEPARATED from the Father that the FATHER stated he was both "**DEAD**" and "**LOST**" at that point (Lk. 15:32)! Spiritual death is separation from God, Eph. 4:18,19. See also **Jam. 1:14,15** on how sin brings forth separation (death). **If certain sins can exclude a Christian from the kingdom, then sin can "SEPARATE" us from God, though not from His love!** Remember this important truth when interpreting Rom. 8:35-39.

In Mk. 9:43-48, Jesus clearly taught that SIN is to be avoided to the extreme, since **sin can send people to eternal Hell fire.** He spoke these words directly to the Twelve Apostles, as verse 35 shows. This makes this passage very similar to Gal. 5:19-21. Why then do the U. E. S. teachers down play sin's potential destructive power by limiting its ability to adversely affect just three areas for the believer in Christ: communion with the Father, taking away the joy of salvation, and losing rewards? For some it could be that they are so concerned with ministry size and numbers, they are appealing to the weak and lukewarm, making them feel good about themselves, while being careful not to say anything that might offend them or cause them to leave and go to another congregation! Such ministers are NOT servants of God and need to repent!

Getting back to the **love of Christ**, we shockingly learn that **Jesus "loved" the Hell-bound, unforgiven, enemy of God and rejecter of truth commonly called the rich, young ruler (Mk. 10:21).** In other words, people who now have the wrath of God abiding on them (Jn. 3:36) are loved by Christ too, as taught here!

Finally, regarding Rom. 8:35-39, Jude 21 says: "**Keep yourselves** in God's love . . . ." [Notice our own **human responsibility** in keeping ourselves in God's love!]

The Apostle Peter wrote: "If they have escaped the corruption of the world by knowing our Lord and Savior Jesus Christ and are again entangled in it and overcome, they are worse off at the end than they were at the beginning. It would have been better for them not to have known the way of righteousness, than to have known it and then to turn their backs on the sacred command that was passed on to them. Of them the proverbs are true: 'A dog returns to its vomit,' and 'A sow that is washed goes back to her wallowing in the mud.' " (2 Pet. 2:20-22).

In spite of its clarity, there are some who say this passage does not refer to a person once saved, who afterwards got entangled again in the pollutions of the world and finally ended up in a lost spiritual condition! Their reasoning is that these were only *"enlightened lost people"* [10] who never did accept Christ. They were always dogs and sows and never became sheep.

First of all, one must carefully consider the context to ascertain how a noun like "sheep" is used. Sometimes "sheep" is **NOT** referring to a saved person at all **(Isa. 53:6)**! The way it is used by Isaiah is to liken mankind to the trait of sheep going astray. Similarly, the way "dog" and "sow" are used by Peter here makes only the point that the people they are likened to **RETURNED TO** sin ("vomit") just like a dog in the natural does; and **WENT BACK** to a completely sinful lifestyle ("wallowing in the mud") just like a female hog in the natural.

Remember, these people in question clearly did, at one point, **"ESCAPE the corruption of the world by knowing our Lord and Savior Jesus Christ."** This is the same kind of description that Peter uses in his second epistle, chapter 1, verses 3 and 4, which means one

IT IS ONLY THROUGH THE BLOOD OF CHRIST THAT ONE CAN ESCAPE SLAVERY TO SIN.

is saved! Also, **it is UNSCRIPTURAL to declare that one can escape the sins of the world and remain unsaved! It is ONLY through the blood of Jesus Christ and his wonderful salvation that one can escape slavery to sin and become free (Jn. 8:34-36; Rev. 1:5b). Regrettably, U. E. S. teachers, in an effort to explain away 2 Pet. 2:20-22, have been forced, therefore, to say that Jesus' blood isn't the only way to "escape the corruption of the world"!**

Furthermore, Peter wrote of people that were **"washed"** before they returned to sin's bondages. **Again, it is only by the blood of Jesus Christ that one is "washed" at the point of forgiveness (1 Cor. 6:11 cf. Rev. 7:14)!**

The spiritual condition of these people went from slaves of depravity to freedom from sin's bondages to slaves of depravity for the second time (2 Pet. 2:19,20).

When they were free from sin they knew "the way of righteousness" (2 Pet. 2:21), which is another way of describing JESUS (Matt. 21:32)! Therefore, Jesus enabled them to "escape" sin's bondages!

Finally, they "turned their backs" on the sacred command (2 Pet. 2:21), which in 1 Jn. 3:23 is shown as "...to believe in the name of his Son, Jesus Christ, and to love one another as he commanded us."

Clearly, for the people Peter wrote of, their latter slavery to sin is WORSE and they, therefore, are unsaved again at this point.

Much more could be written on sin and how it carries with it the potential of ruining the Christian's inheritance of the kingdom, but how could anyone improve upon the Holy Spirit inspired words of Heb. 3:12-14, which seem to be a key in understanding this part of our controversy about what sin can do in the life of a Christian: "See to it, brothers, that none of you has a sinful, unbelieving heart that

"WE HAVE COME TO SHARE IN CHRIST IF WE HOLD FIRMLY TILL THE END THE CONFIDENCE WE HAD AT FIRST."

turns away from the Living God. But encourage one another daily, as long as it is called Today, so that none of you may be hardened by sin's deceitfulness. **We have come to share in Christ IF WE HOLD FIRMLY TILL THE END THE CONFIDENCE WE HAD AT FIRST."** (These verses in Hebrews would be good ones for YOU to memorize on this subject and frequently quote to others.)

In contrast to what you just read, another U. E. S. teacher/author, John MacArthur, wrote:

> *"It is God's omnipotent, sovereign power that guards us and guarantees our final victory. God, the ultimate Judge, has justified us in Christ, made us heirs with Him, and has given us His Spirit to ensure that the good work He started in us will be perfected (Phil. 1:6). He is able to keep us from stumbling, and to make us 'stand in the presence of His glory blameless with great joy' (Jude 24). Not even Satan himself can condemn us (Rom. 8:33), so rather than fearing the loss of our inheritance we should continually rejoice in God's great grace and mercy."* [11]

HUMAN RESPONSIBILITY is often omitted by the U. E. S.

teachers, as you just read, but not from the Bible! Scripture teaches: KEEP YOURSELF PURE (1 Tim. 5:22); KEEP YOURSELF FROM IDOLS (1 Jn. 5:21); SAVE YOURSELF (Acts 2:40; 1 Tim. 4:16); KEEP YOUR LAMPS BURNING (Lk. 12:35); KEEP YOUR SPIRITUAL FERVOR (Rom. 12:11); KEEP YOURSELF FROM BEING POLLUTED BY THE WORLD (Jam. 1:27); KEEP YOUR LIVES FREE FROM THE LOVE OF MONEY AND BE CONTENT WITH WHAT YOU HAVE (Heb. 13:5); BUILD YOURSELVES UP (Jude 20); CLEANSE YOURSELF (2 Tim. 2:21); FAN INTO FLAME (2 Tim. 1:6); DO NOT LET SIN REIGN IN YOUR MORTAL BODY (Rom. 6:12); PUT TO DEATH, THEREFORE, WHATEVER BELONGS TO YOUR EARTHLY NATURE: SEXUAL IMMORALITY, IMPURITY, LUST, EVIL DESIRES AND GREED, WHICH IS IDOLATRY (Col. 3:5); DON'T BE OVERCOME WITH EVIL, BUT OVERCOME EVIL WITH GOOD (Rom. 12:21); PUT ON THE WHOLE ARMOR OF GOD (Eph. 6:11); HUMBLE YOURSELVES (1 Pet. 5:6); GUARD YOUR HEART (Prov. 4:23); WAKE UP! STRENGTHEN WHAT REMAINS AND IS ABOUT TO DIE (Rev. 3:2); HOLD ON TO WHAT YOU HAVE UNTIL I COME (Rev. 2:25); BE FAITHFUL, EVEN TO THE POINT OF DEATH (Rev. 2:10); etc. God won't ever neglect His responsibilities and He is certainly able to keep and guard us, but we can neglect ours, through our own free will, to our eternal loss! Obviously, **the Prodigal was responsible for his own neglect, which led to his "lost" condition.**

In Rev. 21:8, we read, "But the cowardly, the unbelieving, the vile, the murderers, the sexually immoral, those who practice magic arts, the idolaters and all liars - their place will be in the fiery lake of burning sulfur. This is the second death." Please note how clear it is that **"the unbelievers" in Christ are NOT the only group that will be thrown into the lake of fire!** While Jn. 3:18 seems to imply this, other Scriptures supplement that verse with added truth. The cowardly, sexually immoral and all the LIARS, just to mention three, will be there too! **Therefore, for the U. E. S. adherents to say that unbelief in Christ is the ONLY sin that will send one to Hell is both DECEPTIVE and UNSCRIPTURAL!** [Also, unbelief in Christ is <u>NOT</u> blasphemy against the Holy Spirit, as Mk. 3:29,30 clearly shows!]

The Bible ends with a WARNING TO CHRISTIANS, "**I <u>WARN</u> everyone who hears the words of the prophecy of this book:** If **ANYONE** adds anything to them, God will add to them the plagues described in this book. And if **ANYONE** takes words away from this book of prophecy, **GOD WILL TAKE AWAY FROM HIM his share in the tree of life and in the holy city, which are described in this book**," Rev. 22:18,19. It is clear that this warning applies to the saved, for **ONLY can a saved person have taken away from him his share in the tree of life and the holy city, New Jerusalem!**

In Rev. 2:7, we learn that Jesus promises only the ones who **overcome** "the right to eat from the tree of life, which is in the paradise of God." This same person (the overcomer) can later have this negated, according to Rev. 22:18,19! Moreover, only those who have their names "written in the Lamb's book of life" have access to the holy city, New Jerusalem, Rev. 21:27. All others will be thrown into the lake of fire (Rev. 20:15). Yet **one can lose his share to the holy city** if he "takes words away from this book of prophecy," Rev. 22:18,19! Clearly, therefore, the believer's security is conditional and not unconditional.

Finally, the warning of Rev. 22:18,19 was written to everyone who hears the words of the prophecy of the book of Revelation, which certainly included millions of Christians over the centuries, especially since Revelation was directly written to the seven churches in Asia (1:11)! **Just the mere fact that such a WARNING holds a very real danger for Christians disproves the U. E. S. of the believer in Christ.** If U. E. S. was true, such a warning to real Christians could **NEVER** be issued, since it would be an impossibility for them not to inherit the kingdom of God!

II. FALSE DOCTRINE ABOUT SALVATION

Does false doctrine ABOUT SALVATION carry with it the potential of causing one to lose eternal life? Paul, writing to Christians, declared, "Mark my words! I, Paul, tell you that if you let yourselves be circumcised **Christ will be of NO VALUE TO YOU AT ALL.** Again I declare to every man who lets himself be circumcised that he is obligated to obey the whole law. **You who are trying to be JUSTIFIED BY THE LAW have been alienated from Christ; you have fallen away from grace**," Gal. 5:2-4. Clearly, the doctrine of justification (or salvation) is the focal point here.

After Paul left the area of Galatia, these real Christians were actually "deserting" God by turning to a different gospel (1:6) that was preached by people who did "pervert the gospel of Christ" (1:7). It seems that their false salvation message included "observing special days and months and seasons and years" (Gal. 4:10), circumcision

(5:2,3,6,11,12; 6:12-15) and being justified by observing the law (3:10; 5:4). This message carried with it the ultimate danger, even for Christians! Hence, this led to Paul's Holy Spirit inspired anathemas in Gal.1:8,9 for ANYONE who would preach a wrong plan of salvation!

Please reread Gal. 5:2-4 again and focus in upon the following facts: (1) Christ will be of **"NO VALUE" TO THEM AT ALL** if they accept this false salvation plan, even though they were saved in the past. ["No value" at all, therefore, includes their salvation from the lake of fire!] (2) They would be alienated from Christ to the place where they have "fallen away from grace." (You can't fall away from grace if you were never in it to begin with!) Since we are clearly saved by "GRACE" (Eph. 2:8,9), then they would no longer be saved, since they "have fallen away from grace"!

Notice what two U. E. S. authors, David N. Steele and Curtis C. Thomas, jointly wrote in their book, The Five Points of Calvinism, about falling from grace:

> "*The doctrine of the perseverance of the saints does not maintain that all who **profess** the Christian faith are certain of heaven. It is **saints** - those who are set apart by the Spirit - who **persevere** to the end. It is **believers** - those who are given true, living faith in Christ - who are **secure** and safe in Him. Many who profess to believe fall away, but they do not fall from grace for they were never in grace. True believers do fall into temptations, and they do commit grievous sins, but these sins do not cause them to lose their salvation or separate them from Christ*" [12] (emphasis theirs, but bold here is italics in original).

In other words, these U. E. S. teachers are saying that it is impossible for a real Christian to "fall from grace" and NO KIND OF SIN can negate our salvation, in contrast to Paul's God-given report!

The warning you just read from Paul was definitely part of his salvation message declared everywhere! In 1 Cor. 15:1,2 Paul wrote similarly, "Now, brothers, I want to remind you of the gospel I preached to you, which you received and on which you have taken your stand. By this gospel you are saved, **IF you hold firmly to the word I preached to you. OTHERWISE, YOU HAVE BELIEVED IN VAIN.**" Please note **we are saved by the Gospel, BUT ONLY IF WE CONTINUE TO HOLD FIRMLY TO PAUL'S MESSAGE OF GRACE.** IF WE DON'T CONTINUE TO HOLD FIRMLY TO

THE TRUE DOCTRINE OF SALVATION, THEN WE WHO

ARE <u>YOU</u> AWARE OF PAUL'S REPEATED DOCTRINAL WARNING DIRECTED TO CHRISTIANS?

HAVE BELIEVED IN CHRIST "**BELIEVED IN VAIN.**" Only a Christian could "believe in vain," as Paul called it. The Apostle Paul, therefore, could not have believed in U. E. S., as is also evident by this passage.

But what about the other apostles of Christ, did they all teach the same way? The answer is an obvious YES.

Perhaps the clearest similar stand alongside Paul comes from the Apostle John! In 1 Jn. 2:24 John wrote, "See that what you have **HEARD** from the beginning **REMAINS** in you. **<u>IF</u> IT DOES, YOU ALSO WILL REMAIN IN THE SON AND IN THE FATHER.**" Clearly, the context from verse 21 to verse 27 reveals false doctrine being taught by false teachers was John's concern. Notice the conditional word "IF" in verse 24. **John believed a danger existed through false doctrine about salvation that could affect Christians not remaining in Christ and the Father!** Obviously, this apostle wasn't a U. E. S. adherent either!

John also wrote "to the chosen lady and her children" (2 Jn. 1) the following: "<u>Anyone</u> who runs ahead and **DOES NOT CONTINUE IN THE <u>TEACHING</u> OF CHRIST DOES NOT HAVE GOD; WHOEVER CONTINUES** in the teaching has both the Father and the Son," 2 Jn. 9. The implications are obvious - we must "continue" with certain doctrine or we do not have God!

According to these clear Biblical passages about the doctrine of salvation and the necessity of continuing in the truth, **if a true Christian in our day would convert over to a Jehovah's Witness, Mormon, Catholic, Seven-Day Adventist, Apostolic, Church of Christ or any other religious system that teaches a wrong plan of salvation, and believe that plan of salvation, then he/she would "fall from grace" and no longer be saved.**

Scripture clearly disagrees with the U. E. S. teachers who take the opposite view, such as Cal Beisner, who addressed baptismal regeneration:

> *"The conclusion of this study must be that baptismal regeneration teaches 'another gospel' by adding a requirement for salvation which Scripture does not teach.*

> *But does this mean that all members of groups teaching baptismal regeneration are 'accursed' (Galatians 1:8-9)? No. Those who, though they now believe otherwise, began by believing that they were saved entirely by grace through faith remain saved (John 10:27-29; 1 Peter 1:4-9). They are* ***simply in error***" [13] (emphasis ours).

There's an **ETERNAL DIFFERENCE** between the U. E. S. "simply in error" and Paul's "believed in vain" and John's "does not have God"! **[This U. E. S. author, however, is correct about baptismal regeneration (or the concept that water baptism is necessary for salvation) being "another gospel" and, therefore, under the true curse of God.]**

The seriousness of a Christian accepting a false plan of salvation ("another gospel") after his own conversion is not only reflected in the book of Galatians, but also Acts 15. The false message, "Unless you are circumcised, according to the custom taught by Moses, you cannot be saved" (v.1) **was being taught to Christians.** Paul and Barnabas reacted with a "sharp dispute and debate with them" (v.2). Why? Their false message about salvation, if accepted, would cause the already saved to "fall from grace" (Gal. 5:2-4)! **Hence, Paul was being a FAITHFUL shepherd by publicly standing against this false doctrine!**

From this section of our study, it should be clear that SOUND DOCTRINE IS EXTREMELY IMPORTANT, especially when it is related, directly or indirectly, to the salvation message! Regarding doctrine, Paul told Titus, "You MUST teach what is in accord with sound doctrine," Tit. 2:1. Also, one of the Scriptural requirements to be an elder is, "He MUST hold firmly to the trustworthy message as it has been taught, so that he can encourage others by sound doctrine and **refute** those who oppose it" (Tit. 1:9). To do so, therefore, cannot be "divisive" as some label!

III. PERSECUTION

Scripture declares, "Everyone who wants to live a godly life in Christ Jesus **WILL be persecuted**," 2 Tim. 3:12. Also, Jesus said, "...No servant is greater than his master. If they persecuted me, **they WILL persecute you also**," Jn. 15:20. These passages immediately make the subject of persecution very relevant to the Christian!

Regarding this, a very important parable, the Parable of the Sower, declares there are four different types of people who hear the

Word of God. The second type mentioned "believe for a while, but in the **time of testing** they fall away," Lk. 8:13. In Matt. 13:21, the explanation of this type of person is given: "But since he has no root, he lasts only a short time. When **TROUBLE OR PERSECUTION comes because of the word, he quickly falls away."** This type of person does NOT CONTINUE to live spiritually, though there was once life produced by the Word of God, as the context shows.

Please note, therefore, that **persecution does NOT come to build us up or promote growth, as some U. E. S. teachers wrongly proclaim!** The Word of God is given to build us up (Acts 20:32) and for growth (1 Pet. 2:2). **Persecution comes as a "test" (Lk. 8:13 cf. Matt. 13:21; Acts 20:19; Rev. 2:10) which will cause some genuine Christians to "fall away" or die spiritually!** Furthermore, persecution does NOT come to weed out the mere professing believers from the

PERSECUTION IS A "TEST"

real Christians, as others teach! Also, the Scriptural meaning of "fall away" in context is **DIE** as evidenced by the "WITHERED" plants. To "fall away" is equated here with ceasing to "believe." Please notice that the "seed" (or Word of God) produced (spiritual) LIFE, for there was a living plant that afterwards WITHERED, or as Jesus taught, such "**believe for a while**, but in the time of testing, they FALL AWAY." **NOTICE: after they initially believed through the Word of God in such a way as to produce life, THEY CEASED BELIEVING (which is likened unto "withering") because of the PERSECUTION OR TROUBLE THAT CAME FROM THE WORD OF GOD IN THEIR LIVES. Clearly then, persecution for godly living can potentially be spiritually fatal to the real Christian!**

Again, from the Parable of the Sower, **please note that it is possible for a Christian to have a genuine, life-producing faith that DOESN'T CONTINUE, as evident in Jesus' words, "believe for a while."** The U. E. S. teachers are wrong to say it was *"a false faith"* that such people had, since it didn't endure. **How could a false faith produce spiritual life?**

Similarly, The N. I. V. Study Bible in its notes on Lk. 8:13 is wrong when it states:

> *This kind of belief is superficial and does not save. It is similar to what James calls 'dead' (Jas 2:17,26) or 'useless' faith (Jas 2:20)."* [14]

Please know that the point made by Jesus, regarding this type of person, is that there was **real life produced by the Word of God that didn't endure, but died because of persecution that befalls the godly.** It wasn't a "dead" faith, as James 2 mentions, for it produced genuine spiritual life until the persecution came and the spiritual life was terminated. In other words, **it wasn't a "dead" faith, but a living faith that became dead!** [BEWARE: Besides The N. I. V. Study Bible, unfortunately, other study Bibles (and reference Bibles) slip in U. E. S. from time to time. The Ryrie Study Bible is another example of such.[15]]

Matt. 24:9,10 is another passage which teaches us about the potential danger of persecution. Jesus said at the end of this age His disciples will be "handed over to be **persecuted** and put to death, and you will be hated by all nations because of me. At that time, **MANY WILL TURN AWAY FROM THE FAITH** and will betray and hate each other." **WHY will "many" turn away from the faith? Because they were persecuted for being Christians.** Also, verses 12 and 13 say, "Because of the increase of wickedness, the love of most will grow cold, but **he who stands firm TO THE END will be saved.**"

> **JESUS TAUGHT IT TWICE, THAT IS, UNLESS WE ENDURE TO THE END WE WILL NOT BE SAVED!**

Matt. 10:21,22 is very similar. These verses read, "Brother will betray brother to death, and a father his child; children will rebel against their parents and have them put to death. All men will hate you because of me, **BUT HE WHO STANDS FIRM TO THE END WILL BE SAVED.**"

Furthermore, Matt. 10:21,22 was spoken to real Christians - the Twelve. **Though they were already saved, they would have to ENDURE (any and all persecutions) TO THE END TO BE SAVED, according to the ultimate teaching authority!**

Jesus declared this powerful truth **TWICE**, that is, about the necessity of us enduring till **THE END** of our lives to be saved (Matt. 10:22; 24:13), yet many with Bibles in our day are **unaware** of it! In contrast, Jesus spoke the truth cited in Jn. 10:27,28 **only once**, yet multitudes of professing Christians know the last half of this passage like they know their names! How sad!

Reader, to learn the whole truth, read and reread the entire New Testament for yourself carefully! Don't just rely upon a favorite teacher, author or even a family member, though sincere, to inform you, for he/she might be wrong!

Scripture declares that a Christian who renounces his/her faith in Jesus during a time of persecution will lose his soul, as just cited.

In response to Matt. 24:13, John R. Rice wrote the following:

> *"To the **careless reader**, this Scripture seems to teach that salvation depends upon holding out faithfully or enduring to the end. But if you read carefully the chapter, you will see that Jesus is talking about the Great Tribulation period at the end of this age, that **the salvation mentioned is salvation of the flesh, not salvation of the soul.** Verse 21 says, 'For then shall be great tribulation, such as was not since the beginning of the world to this time, no, nor ever shall be.' This time mentioned here is the Great Tribulation time. And verse 22 says, 'and except those days should be shortened, there should no flesh be saved.' The salvation mentioned here is the salvation of the flesh, that is, **the rescue of literal Jews from physical death during the Great Tribulation.** Take the Bible at face value. You see that this Scripture does not **teach salvation by works** or by holding out faithfully. To those Jews who will be so terribly persecuted in the tribulation period Jesus said in effect, 'If you are able to endure these persecutions to the end of the tribulation period, I will come and rescue you out of the hands of the Antichrist' "* [16] (emphasis ours).

John Rice not only falsely accuses his opponent of being a "*careless reader*" if he/she differs with him about the interpretation of Matt. 24:13, but also, most seriously, concludes that such who differ "*teach salvation by works*"! If this was true, then **EVERY** person who understood this verse as meaning Christians must remain faithful to the end of their lives without disowning Jesus to inherit God's kingdom, is unsaved! This is the logical conclusion, based on Eph. 2:8,9 cf. Rom. 11:6. **Rice leaves no room for the CAREFUL READER of Scripture, who believes we are saved by grace apart from all works, yet believes our salvation can be negated during a time of persecution by disowning Christ!**

John Rice, in his explanation of Matt. 24:13, somehow neglected to mention that Matt. 10:21-23 is a parallel passage which has the **SAME EXACT WORDING**: "He who stands firm to the end will be saved" and carries with its context hatred, betrayal, and persecution "**because of me [Jesus]**" just like Matt. 24:9-13! Please note that this hatred, betrayal, and persecution is **BECAUSE OF CHRIST** in **BOTH** passages (Matt. 10:22; 24:9)! Therefore, this is NOT trouble coming on the "*literal Jews*," as Rice says, but **trouble coming on disciples of Christ because they are Christians** as Matt. 10:22 shows with crystal clarity! It is **IMPOSSIBLE** for his "*literal Jews*" interpretation of "he who stands firm to the end will be saved" to fit Matt. 10:22! He has read into Scripture something that is not there, because of his doctrinal biases. Like many who firmly embrace U. E. S., Dr. Rice must come up with some answer, as absurd as it may be, to defend his beloved, mythological doctrine, though he must neglect a parallel passage with the **SAME EXACT WORDING** and overlook the clear, explanatory words "**because of me**" in Matt. 24:9 to do so! This is bad enough but he goes even further by saying people, like this author, are "*teaching salvation by works*" in an effort to immediately discredit all vocal Christians who hold to a conditional security for the believer!

Paul wanted Timothy to repeat certain basic spiritual truths frequently to Christians as 2 Tim. 2:11-14 reveals. Verse 12 reads, "If we endure, we will also reign. **IF WE DISOWN HIM, HE WILL ALSO DISOWN US**." Please note that Paul knew a real Christian could **DISOWN** Jesus! (Peter had done this three consecutive times because of fear of persecution, Matt. 26:34.) NOTE: **one can't "DISOWN" something or someone unless he first owned it**! In other

HOW CAN WE STILL BE SAVED IF JESUS "DISOWNS" US?

words, Jesus could not "disown" us unless we first "belonged" to him, which is only possible if one is a Christian (Rom. 14:8; Gal. 5:24). **PAUL'S GRACE TEACHING was, if we would DISOWN Jesus, He in turn would DISOWN us, the same as what the Lord himself warned on more than one occasion before the cross (Matt. 10:33; Lk. 12:9)**! [Dr. Robert Young, in his Analytical Concordance, renders this Greek word as: "*To deny, **disown***" [17] (emphasis ours).] Also, note from 2 Tim. 2:12 that we must ENDURE now to reign with Jesus in the future. Furthermore, reigning with Christ in the future is for ALL Christians, not just some (Rev. 20:6; 22:5)! Therefore, **we must ENDURE any and all types of persecutions to be an overcomer and enter God's kingdom. It is NOT an automatic guarantee after salvation!** Jesus said, "To him who overcomes and **DOES MY WILL TO THE END**, I will give authority over the nations," Rev. 2:26.

Regarding Peter's denial of Jesus, Luke 22:31,32 is sometimes used by the U. E. S. adherents to weaken the force of it. These verses read, "Simon, Simon, Satan has asked to sift you as wheat. But I have prayed for you, that your faith may not fail. And **when you have turned back**, strengthen your brothers." It is suggested that Peter's faith didn't really fail, even though he denied Jesus, because of Jesus' prayer for him. However, the words "when you **HAVE TURNED BACK**" seems to be overlooked by them. Remember, **one can't "turn back" unless he first turned away!** The literal Greek is "having turned." Also, the Greek word used here is the same Greek word found in Acts 3:19; 28:27; and Jam. 5:20 when TURNING is used in reference to salvation! The K. J. V. uses the word "converted" in Lk. 22:32. (Regarding Jesus' powerful prayer for Peter, please see explanation under Objection #13 in the chapter entitled, U. E. S. Arguments and Proof Texts.)

In an effort to weaken the force of 2 Tim. 2:12, the U. E. S. teachers apply a faulty interpretation to the next verse (v.13): "If we are faithless, he will remain faithful, for he cannot disown himself." **What does it mean that God "cannot DISOWN himself "? Clearly, it doesn't mean Jesus won't "disown" us, if we DISOWN Him, for it has been cited three times that He definitely will!** What is the meaning, then, in context? It means that God WILL BE "FAITHFUL" TO HIS WORD TO DISOWN US, AS WE ARE WARNED, even though we show ourselves, at the time, unfaithful to our word by disowning Jesus during our test of persecution! If God didn't disown the one who disowns Him, He would actually be "disowning himself" by not being faithful to his warning to do so!

Rev. 2:10,11 spoken by the ascended and glorified Lord of Glory is also clear about persecution: "Do not be afraid of what you are about to suffer. I tell you, the devil will put some of you in prison to **TEST** you, and you will **SUFFER PERSECUTION** for ten days. **BE FAITHFUL, EVEN TO THE POINT OF DEATH, AND I WILL GIVE YOU THE CROWN OF LIFE.** He who has an ear, let him hear what the Spirit says to the churches. **HE WHO OVERCOMES WILL NOT BE HURT AT ALL BY THE SECOND DEATH.**" We must overcome any suffering and even death through persecution to be faithful to the end. **Only he who "overcomes" or is approved after this "TEST" won't be hurt by the second death!** (The second death is the lake of fire, Rev. 21:8.) This warning was issued directly to the Christians in Smyrna, a very good church in Asia Minor at that time! Ponder this stirring truth spoken by Jesus AFTER His death on the cross.

A similar type of warning is cited by Jesus to His followers in Matt. 10:28, "Do not be afraid of those who kill the body but cannot kill the soul. Rather, **be afraid** of the One who can destroy both soul and body in Hell." Implied is the danger that persecution could cause us to disown Christ, thereby forcing God to disown us. Consequently, our souls and bodies would be cast into the lake of fire.

The days surrounding the reign of the Antichrist will be filled with idolatry, demon worship, murder, etc. (Rev. 9:20,21). When the image of the beast is the focal point of worship the false prophet will "cause all who refused to worship the image to be killed" (Rev. 13:15). About the same time, the mark of the beast will be issued,

WHEN HEADS START TO ROLL

which will be needed to buy or sell anything (Rev. 13:16,17). Decapitation will be the form of execution used at this future time (Rev. 20:4,5). Imagine what it will be like then when the heads of the faithful Christians start to roll!

Now with all this in mind, focus in upon Rev. 14:9-11, "A third angel followed them and said in a loud voice: 'If anyone worships the beast and his image and receives his mark on the forehead or on the hand, he, too, will drink of the wine of God's fury, which has been poured full strength into the cup of his wrath. He will be tormented with burning sulfur in the presence of the holy angels and of the Lamb. And the smoke of their torment rises for ever and ever. There is no rest day or night for those who worship the beast and his image, or for anyone who receives the mark of his name.' "

Will Christians be there at this point in time? **YES**, according to verse 12: "This calls for patient endurance on the part of **the saints who obey God's commandments and REMAIN FAITHFUL TO JESUS.**" Please note that the saints who do NOT "remain faithful to Jesus," that is, they receive the mark of the beast and worship his image - their future is described as **"tormented with burning sulfur...the smoke of their torment rises for ever and ever...no rest day or night."** Again, we see from this passage that **persecution, or just the fear of being persecuted, can be spiritually fatal for some Christians! Hence, there cannot be U. E. S. for the believer in Christ!**

3

⁂ Fourteen Biblical Examples ⁂

In a tract written by a U. E. S. teacher, the author, in disbelief to the opposing position, wrote: "*Show me one man in the Scriptures who was saved and then lost.*"[18] The following section of this study will cite fourteen examples!

I. Demas

Demas was a traveling companion of the Apostle Paul (Col. 4:14; Philemon 24). Together they worked, enduring various troubles and persecution, to extend the kingdom of God. However, in Paul's last letter before his own martyrdom, he informed Timothy of the following change in Demas: "For DEMAS, because **he loved this world**, has deserted me and has gone to Thessalonica" (2 Tim. 4:10).

The Wuest expanded translation reads: "Demas let me down, having set a high value upon this present age and thus **has come to love it.**" This translation clearly states that at the time of Demas' departure from Paul: (1) He "LOVED this world" which caused him to desert Paul. **[The Greek shows what Demas came to love is what Satan is god of (2 Cor. 4:4)!]** (2) He didn't love the "world" like this earlier in his Christian life. In other words, his heart condition was, at the time of Paul's last letter, **different!**

Remembering all this about Demas, let Scripture speak to you more extensively about him: "Do not love the world or anything in the world. **If ANYONE loves the world, the love of the Father is not in him,**" 1 Jn. 2:15. The seriousness of not loving the Father is evident from Jam. 1:12; 2:5 and Jn. 5:42. In other words, this reflects that **one is NOT saved when he doesn't love the Father.** This is what Demas degenerated to.

Though there are two different Greek words used in the original language and translated "world" in 2 Tim. 4:10 and 1 Jn. 2:15, the close relationship between the two is easily seen in Eph. 2:1,2: "As for you, you were dead in your transgressions and sins, in which you used to live when you followed the **WAYS** of this **WORLD** and of the ruler of the kingdom of the air, the spirit who is now at work in those who are disobedient." The word translated, "WAYS" is the same word found in 2 Tim. 4:10, which is also what Demas came to love. The word translated, "WORLD" is the same word found in 1 Jn. 2:15!

Jam. 4:4 supplements all this by adding: "You adulterous people, don't you know that **friendship with the world is hatred toward God? Anyone who chooses to be a friend of the world BECOMES an enemy of God**." James was writing to a group of spiritual adulterers. (Compare this to Jer. 3:20 and Ezek. 6:9.) Notice how James declares that **one can BECOME an enemy of God.** One is either saved or unsaved; with Jesus or against him; a child of God or an enemy of God. Now, for one to "**become an enemy of God**" must imply he was, just before that spiritual condition, a child of God. There is no other spiritual condition to be

ONE CAN BECOME AN ENEMY OF GOD [AGAIN]!

in! **So if one "becomes" an enemy of God from his former spiritual condition of being saved, then he/she can't be saved any more!** In other words, James cites in condensed form what we just read earlier, that is, **a Christian can come to love the world and show himself no longer saved**. He also described what happened to Demas! This is also the answer for those who say, based on the Old Testament, that "Christ is married to the backslider," but fail to say, "**I gave faithless Israel her CERTIFICATE OF DIVORCE and sent her away BECAUSE OF ALL HER ADULTERIES,**" Jer. 3:8!

II. The Prodigal Son

The Prodigal Son also clearly refutes both strands of U. E. S. In Lk. 15:11-32, we learn that the younger of two sons desired to depart from the Father's presence and be with the prostitutes. After he spent all his money and was in great distress, he "came to his senses." He then turned from his sins (repented), was willing to admit that he had sinned and went back into the presence of the Father to work for (or serve) him. This resulted in a feast of celebration. The Father said, "Bring the fattened calf and kill it. Let's have a feast and celebrate. **For this son of mine WAS DEAD and is ALIVE AGAIN; he WAS LOST and is FOUND**," verses 23 and 24. See also verse 32.

From this teaching of Jesus we learn: (1) A genuine "son" can die spiritually because of sinning. (2) No man "plucked" the Prodigal out of the Father's hand, but the Father let him walk away to his own spiritual harm to the place where he was "lost." (3) He was "sealed" until the day of redemption like other children of God, but he still DIED and BECAME LOST because of sexual immorality. (4) The Father didn't "leave" or "forsake" him, but he LEFT and FORSOOK the Father! (5) He became "**alive again**" which implies his spiritual condition went as follows: SPIRITUALLY ALIVE - then SPIRITUALLY DEAD or LOST - then SPIRITUALLY "ALIVE AGAIN." This also means he got saved **AGAIN** after he repented. [This is similar to Rom. 11:23, "And if they do not persist in unbelief, they will be grafted in, for God is able to **GRAFT THEM IN AGAIN**."]

"Once a son, always a son. Therefore, we can't ever become 'lost,' " some say. In contrast, the Father described the Prodigal Son's spiritual condition as both "DEAD" and "LOST" when he was in unrepentant sin with the prostitutes! **Remember 1 Cor. 6:9,10.**

Furthermore, consider the implications of Deut. 32:5 written about Israel which reads, "They have acted corruptly toward him; to their shame **THEY ARE NO LONGER HIS CHILDREN**, but a warped and crooked generation."

Finally, remember Ezek. 33:12,13, "Therefore, son of man, say to your countrymen, 'the righteousness of the righteous man will not save him when he disobeys, and the wickedness of the wicked man will not cause him to fall when he turns from it. The righteous man, if he sins, will not be allowed to live because of his former righteousness.' If I tell the righteous man that he will surely live, but then he trusts in his righteousness and does evil, none of the righteous things he has done will be remembered; he will die for the evil he has done."

Two such examples of this are Solomon and Manasseh. The former turned from his righteousness to do evil (1 Ki. 11:4,9), while the latter turned from his wickedness to do righteousness (2 Chron. 33). **THERE IS NO SENIORITY WITH GOD! IT'S YOUR FINAL SPIRITUAL CONDITION THAT COUNTS! You MUST "ENDURE" till the end of your life. You MUST CONTIN-**

UE TO BELIEVE ON JESUS CHRIST or be **"LOST."**

III. Judas Iscariot

Judas Iscariot was, at one time, both an apostle (Matt. 10:2) and **a "disciple" of Christ (Matt. 10:1)**. Jesus, however, declared that he ended up in the torments of Hell fire with the words, "...But woe to the man who betrays the Son of Man! **It would be better for him if he had not been born**" (Mk. 14:21b). [Obviously, this can't be implying "Paradise" as mentioned in Lk. 23:43 and 2 Cor. 12:4.] These truths have caused great trouble for the U. E. S. adherents, for it is a clear denunciation of their doctrine by the Lord Himself!

Some try to escape the force of these combined verses by saying one can be a disciple of Christ, like Judas, yet never be a real follower of Christ. However, Lk. 14:27 declares this is impossible with the words: **"and anyone who does not carry his cross and follow me CANNOT BE MY DISCIPLE."** Also, Jesus taught, "... **Any of you who does not give up everything he has CANNOT BE MY DISCIPLE,"** Lk. 14:33. Judas Iscariot met all these conditions of commitment to Christ, just as much as the rest of the Twelve, since he too was indeed a "disciple" as they were.

Others will say Judas was called a "devil" (Jn. 6:70), a "thief" (Jn. 12:6), and "Satan entered into him" (Jn. 13:27), how then could he have been saved? **Such overlook the truth that one's spiritual condition can CHANGE from righteous to evil as we clearly saw with Demas, the Prodigal Son and Solomon.** Yes, Judas was once saved, though he wasn't "clean" shortly before the betrayal (Jn. 13:10,11)! **This, however, does NOT mean he was NEVER SAVED!** Remember, **Judas was clearly the Lord's "disciple" in the beginning!**

Some have also confused the truth stated in Jn. 6:64 to mean Judas NEVER believed, even from the beginning. However, it doesn't say this at all! The verse reads, " 'Yet there are some of you who do not believe.' For Jesus had known from the beginning which of **them** (plural) did not believe and **who** (singular) would betray him." Notice there are TWO groups referred to here. This is evident in the Greek. One is plural in tense that didn't believe from the beginning and the other is singular in tense referring to Judas who would betray him! The Wuest translation renders Jn. 6:64 as follows: "But there are certain of you who are not believing. For Jesus knew from the beginning who **THEY WERE**

who were not believing, and **who the ONE WAS who was betraying Him." Remember, Judas was once a "disciple." He must have believed at the beginning!**

Matthias was the apostolic replacement for Judas, as we read: "To take the place in this ministry and receive the position of an apostle from which Judas **fell away and went astray** to go (where he belonged), to his own (proper) place," Acts 1:25, Amplified Bible. Judas "went astray" from his former condition.

In Matt. 10, we have a number of directives given by the Lord to the entire Twelve, **including Judas.** Verse 25 implies Jesus was Judas' "head" and Judas was a member of Jesus' "household"! Verse 29 also declares God to be the spiritual "Father" of Judas, at that point in time. To "receive" Judas, before he "went astray" - when he was still a "disciple," was the same as "receiving" Jesus, verse 40. When Judas would be arrested for preaching God's Word, he wasn't to worry on what or how he was to answer for the Spirit of the Father would speak through him, verse 20. Also, Judas was a servant of God and Jesus was his Master, verse 24. **Also, if Judas was never saved then Jesus sent him, like the rest of the Twelve, to preach his message, heal the sick, raise the dead, cleanse leprosy and drive out demons (Matt. 10:7,8)! Would Jesus give an unsaved man the same type of spiritual authority (verse 1) along with the unquestionably saved apostles, to likewise be his holy representative? NEVER! Also, please note the high spiritual qualifications listed in 1 Tim. 3:1-7 and Tit. 1:7-9 which a spiritual leader, like Judas, had to meet! In fact, Judas had a higher office as apostle than these! See Eph. 4:11.**

Judas was once a saved man who preached the Gospel, healed the sick, then "went astray" and ended up in Hell, after he betrayed Jesus and committed suicide.

In Jn. 17:12 we read, "While I was with them, I protected them and kept them safe by that name you gave me. **None has been lost <u>EXCEPT</u> the one doomed to destruction so that Scripture would be fulfilled."** This passage also teaches Judas was once saved, for he became "lost." (If he was never saved he would have always been in the category of "lost.")

Also, Jn. 17:12 is similar to someone saying the following: "Here are the twelve marbles you gave me. NONE HAS BEEN LOST <u>EXCEPT</u> THE ONE green marble." Would that statement mean that he never had twelve marbles to begin with? Or, could it mean that the green marble (likened unto Judas) was never in his possession, even at the beginning? Of course not! Why do some read Scripture that way? **If Judas was never saved, he couldn't be the EXCEPTION to the other eleven who were kept safe!**

Finally, please notice the obvious conclusion we must come to by comparing Jn. 17:2 to Jn. 17:12. Jesus gave **eternal life** to all the Father "gave" him, v. 2. Clearly, Judas is included in this group of recipients as v. 12 shows! Therefore, Judas once had eternal life like the rest of the Twelve!

Suicide was just mentioned in conjunction with Judas. With its growth today, especially among teens, this subject needs to be briefly addressed.

Many large U. E. S. ministries have been asked, "If a Christian commits suicide will he still go to Heaven?" Unfortunately, their answer to this question over coast to coast radio and in their

IF A CHRISTIAN COMMITS SUICIDE, WILL HE STILL GO TO HEAVEN?

literature is almost always disturbing, and all because of the implications of their doctrine! One exception to this is D. James Kennedy, who embraces the moderate view of U. E. S., and who wrote the following: "*Judas, in his apostasy,* ***committed suicide, and thus demonstrated that he was not truly a believer***" [19] (emphasis ours). [Certainly, Judas was not a Christian at the point of his suicide. **However, that doesn't mean he NEVER was, which has already been proven Scripturally!**]

Another teacher who needs to be cited is Jack Hayford. Though he often sounds like a U. E. S. proponent, he does not accept it. In spite of this, however, he overlooks Rev. 21:8 and 1 Jn. 3:15b to embrace his compromised position on suicide:

> "*That I want everyone to understand that* ***it is error to suppose that simply because a person commits suicide, they therefore have lost their eternal soul,*** *that having said that does not mean it is not possible for a person to lose their soul when they've been saved. But it is an extremely demanding and difficult thing to lose your soul. If you want to, you can do it. It can be done. And there are people that have done it*" [20] (emphasis ours).

One can only wonder how many premature deaths resulted as a

consequence of this and other similar teachings about suicide; or even worse, how many went to Hell!

Remember this: like abortion, "suicide" is just another name for MURDER. However, to be more exact, **suicide is SELF-MURDER**! But even beyond this, **it is the kind of murder one can NOT repent of!** Unlike Paul and David, who murdered others but were later forgiven, suicide victims can NOT find forgiveness! Be not deceived, ALL unforgiven "murderers," without exception, will end up in the lake of fire (Rev. 21:8; 1 Jn. 3:15b), even if that one was once saved, then committed suicide because of a bad combination, that is, painful circumstances, hopelessness and a belief in unconditional eternal security!

Some have tried to excuse the sin of suicide (self-murder) with the following rationale: "*If one is mentally ill, he isn't responsible for his actions.*" **To excuse any sin this way, including self-murder, is NOT Scriptural. There is absolutely NO Biblical backing for such a statement!** Besides, mental illness isn't the root of sin, the **heart** of man is! Jesus said: "What comes out of a man is what makes him 'unclean.' For from **within, out of men's HEARTS** come evil thoughts, sexual immorality, theft, **MURDER**, adultery, greed, malice, deceit, lewdness, envy, slander, arrogance and folly. All these evils come from inside and make a man 'unclean,' " Mk. 7:20-23. **Please note that MURDER (which includes suicide) comes from the HEART of sinful man and is not a mental illness!**

Some Christians will be, and in fact are now, heavily distressed over their personal circumstances. Subtly, the devil has given the U. E. S. adherent the idea to escape their problems through suicide and go to Heaven. However, U. E. S. is **FALSE**. Therefore, they won't be going to Heaven, since they committed the soul-damning sin of **MURDER** and couldn't repent of it! It is vitally important that suicide, like other satanic temptations, be steadfastly resisted. In other words, **don't even for a moment entertain suicidal thoughts**. Such Christians that yield to this temptation will only be intensifying their pain and misery in eternity, not escaping it!

IV. Simon

Simon, who once "practiced sorcery" in a city in Samaria (Acts 8:5-9), was influenced spiritually by Philip, the evangelist, but later needed to repent because his heart wasn't right. But was he ever saved? Yes, according to verse 13! There we learn that "**Simon**

himself believed"! This settles the question once and for all! He "believed" like the others in that city who believed and were baptized, verse 12. In fact, Simon too received Christian baptism! However, sometime after the point that Simon "believed," **Peter declared that his HEART wasn't right before God and he needed to repent at that time, verses 21 and 22.** This declaration by Peter, however, doesn't mean that Simon was never saved, for Scripture declares that he did, indeed, "believe"! **The belief Simon had qualified him for Christian baptism, just as the Ethiopian eunuch was qualified for baptism after he believed, Acts 8:34-39.** Remember, one can believe for "a while" and quickly "fall away" through persecution (Lk. 8:13). Though persecution isn't even implied in Simon's short walk with the Lord, he still, likewise, "believed," then needed to repent of sin afterwards (v.23).

V. Hymenaeus and Philetus

Hymenaeus and Philetus were first-century apostates. 2 Tim. 2:17,18 read: "Their teaching will spread like gangrene. Among them are Hymenaeus and Philetus, **who have wandered away from the truth**. They say that the resurrection has already taken place, and **they destroy the faith of some**." Notice the following:

First, they "wandered away from the truth." One can't "wander away from the truth" unless he is first in "the truth," which is a description of Jesus (Jn. 14:6)!

Though we know very little about Philetus, perhaps we have a shade more information about HYMENAEUS. In 1 Tim. 1:19,20, Hymenaeus, if the same person, is mentioned as a person who "shipwrecked" HIS FAITH. This is cited as a warning to Timothy to hold on to the "faith and a good conscience" which Hymenaeus (and Alexander) didn't do. This shows that they were once saved, as Timothy was, when he got this word of caution from Paul.

Secondly, Hymenaeus and Philetus were **DESTROYING THE FAITH of unnamed Christian people that Paul knew of by their teaching** about the resurrection! The ones adversely affected by their teaching must have been Christians, for their FAITH WAS DESTROYED! Certain false doctrines, if believed, can do this to real Christians, as already cited!

VI. Many Unnamed Disciples

Many unnamed disciples of Jn. 6:66 fell away and went to Hell.

That verse is clear and needs no additional comments: "From that time **many of his DISCIPLES turned back and NO LONGER FOLLOWED HIM.**" Remember Lk. 14:27,33 when understanding their prior commitment to Jesus.

The U. E. S. position that a backslider will always come back to the Lord is clearly refuted by Jn. 6:66. Furthermore, Saul, King of Israel, and Judas Iscariot both backslid and **clearly never came back to the Lord**! With this in mind, how do we answer the U. E. S. argument from Matt. 18:12-14 that none of Christ's sheep that wander off, will in the end, perish? Verse 13 reads, "**And if he finds it**, I tell you the truth, he is happier about the one sheep than about the ninety-nine that did not wander off." This verse qualifies the U. E. S. position by stating: "**If he finds it**." Therefore, the possibility of not being brought back exists and is conditional upon us being found! Finally, if we interpret Scripture with Scripture, this is the only conclusion we can logically come to, especially with Jn. 6:66 in mind.

VII. Some Younger Christian Widows

Some younger Christian widows turned from Jesus and started to follow Satan! 1 Tim. 5:14,15 read, "So I counsel younger widows to marry, to have children, to manage their homes and to give the enemy no opportunity for slander. **Some have in fact already TURNED AWAY TO FOLLOW SATAN.**" Please note that one can NOT "TURN AWAY to FOLLOW SATAN" unless he/she was first following someone else! Since there is only one other possibility, they must have been following Jesus before they turned to start to follow Satan! According to verse 11, this awful event occurred "**...when their sensual desires overcame their DEDICATION TO CHRIST....**" Clearly, it is stated that they did have a real "dedication to Christ" at first, which died. Then they started to "follow Satan."

In contrast to Paul, many U. E. S. proponents if present then, would have been forced to comment that those widows were NEVER REALLY SAVED TO BEGIN WITH <u>or</u> forfeit their beloved doctrine!

VIII. Some Christians "Eager For Money"

Some Christians "eager for money" have wandered from the Christian faith! Paul wrote, "But if we have food and clothing, we will **be content** with that. People who want to get rich fall into temptation and a trap and into many foolish and harmful desires that plunge men into **RUIN AND DESTRUCTION.** For the love of money is a root of all kinds of evil. **SOME PEOPLE, EAGER FOR MONEY, HAVE WANDERED FROM THE FAITH and pierced themselves with many griefs**" (1 Tim. 6:8-10). Please note the words "**RUIN AND DESTRUCTION.**" The same Greek word as found here in v.9 is also used in Matt. 7:13 and rendered "destruction," which clearly refers to Hell: "...For wide is the gate and broad is the road that leads to **destruction**, and many enter through it."

This section of Holy Writ is especially relevant in the United States today, with its rampant sin of GREED, that is, an ever-increasing desire for more. God only knows how many Christians have "wandered from the faith" in our own generation, back into darkness and a mind dominated by earthly things and sinful desires. The deceitfulness of wealth is likened unto "thorns" in the soil of our heart, which can have a deadly influence (Mk. 4:18,19).

We should all ponder long what Jesus said about the rich: "It is easier for a camel to go through the eye of a needle than for a rich man to enter the kingdom of God," Lk. 18:25.

Paul's report about these false teachers is that they are "men of corrupt mind, who have been robbed of the truth." Their message was "**godliness is a means to financial gain,**" 1 Tim. 6:5. What a clear refutation this verse is (along with the next six verses) to another popular, but false, teaching of our day known as The Prosperity Message as taught by Kenneth and Gloria Copeland, Kenneth Hagin, Robert Tilton, Jerry Savelle, Fred Price, Marilyn Hickey, Charles Capps and others. What a subtle, inherent danger is lurking in The Prosperity Message which breeds covetousness, a type of **idolatry** (Col. 3:5)!

Heb. 13:5 commands, "**Keep your lives free from the love of money and BE CONTENT with what you have....**"

A good prayer for us all to pray regarding temporal possessions is found in Prov. 30:8,9: "**...Give me neither poverty nor riches, but GIVE ME ONLY MY DAILY BREAD. Otherwise, I may have too much and disown you and say, 'Who is the Lord?' Or I may become poor and steal, and so dishonor the name of my God.**"

Reader, do YOU have the heart to sincerely pray this prayer?

IX. Fruitless Christians

Fruitless Christians are in the greatest danger. Unless they repent and bear "fruit," they will be severed from Christ and will be "thrown into the fire and burned," according to Jesus! What a shock it must be to some to hear statements like this, but Jesus taught this truth more than once!

In Jn. 15:2, Jesus taught about the Father, "He **cuts off** every branch **IN ME** that bears no fruit, while every branch that does bear fruit he trims clean so that it will be even more fruitful." (Notice how the Father wants "fruit.") What happens to people that do NOT "REMAIN" in Christ (the "branches" that get cut off because they bear no fruit)? Verse 6 gives the answer, "**If anyone does not remain in me, he is like a branch that is thrown away and withers; such branches are picked up, THROWN INTO THE FIRE AND BURNED.**" Remember this: **Jesus taught in Jn. 15:1-10 that there are two types of Christians - those that DO "REMAIN" in Him and bring forth fruit and those that DO NOT REMAIN (the fruitless) and end up in the fire!** [Though U. E. S. teaches that a real Christian **must** "remain," the Lord taught otherwise!] The K.J.V. uses the word "abide" in this passage instead of "remain." The reader should be aware that the Greek meaning of "abide" is REMAIN!

Matt. 25:14-30 is commonly called the Parable of the Talents. The servant of the Master who was entrusted with one talent **GAINED** ABSOLUTELY NOTHING. His Master returned from his journey and called him to account. The Master of that servant then said, "**And throw that worthless servant outside, into the darkness, WHERE THERE WILL BE WEEPING AND GNASHING OF TEETH,**" verse 30. Only a Christian can be expected to gain from what was given him.

Finally, in Lk. 13:6-9, Jesus taught about a fruit tree that wasn't bearing fruit. The owner of the vineyard went to it for three years without finding any. It would be given just one more year to bear fruit - with special attention of digging around it and being fertilized - then **it would be CUT DOWN (or KILLED), if it remained fruitless**!

X. The "Servant" Who Backslides in Lk. 12

The "servant" who backslides to the point where he "begins" to beat others and get drunk is another example. Read Lk. 12:45,46. Notice, he "BEGAN" to do evil acts as he pondered the long-time delay in his Master's return. Was that "servant" unconditionally eternally secure? **Not according to Jesus!** Verse 46 reads, "The master of that servant will come on a day when he does not expect him and at an hour he is not aware of. He will cut him to pieces and **assign him a place WITH THE UNBELIEVERS.**" The "place with the unbelievers" is clearly shown to be **THE FIERY LAKE OF BURNING SULFUR**, according to Rev. 21:8. Also, **NO unrepentant drunkard, like that servant, will inherit the kingdom of God, 1 Cor. 6:9,10; Gal. 5:19-21. (This is true even if he was once a faithful servant!) It is, therefore, IMPOSSIBLE TO BE A DRUNKARD AND A CHRISTIAN AT THE SAME TIME, in contrast to what some would like to believe!**

XI. The Unrepentant Lukewarm

The Unrepentant Lukewarm, so rampant in our day, are issued a very straightforward warning by the Lord Himself! When Jesus addressed this issue in Rev. 3:14-22, those lukewarm Christians WERE STILL SAVED AT THAT MOMENT. However, such people will be rebuked and disciplined by God unless they repent. If after this, they still refuse to become "hot," then Jesus will spit them out of His mouth! **In other words, they will no longer be in the body of Christ!** One must overcome the tendency to stay lukewarm because of life's struggles, disappointments and problems, that even befall the godly, to have the right to sit with Jesus on His throne, v.21. Jesus Himself declared this! [Yet to come is a whole chapter devoted to lukewarmness.]

XII. The Unforgiving in Heart

The unforgiving in heart will nullify their own forgiveness, according to the ultimate authority - the Lord Jesus! The Father forgiving us of our sins is **CONDITIONAL** upon our own forgiving of others who have sinned against us! Jesus taught, "For <u>if</u> you forgive men when they sin against you, your heavenly Father will also forgive you. **But <u>if</u> you do not forgive men their sins, your FATHER will not forgive your sins** (Matt. 6:14,15)." This can only

FORGIVE OTHERS OR NULLIFY YOUR OWN FORGIVENESS!

be referring to the saved, for the unsaved have the devil as their spiritual father (Jn. 8:44)!

Also, Jesus elaborated on this important subject of forgiving others at another time when Peter asked him about the number of times he should forgive his brother who sins against him. Read over **Matt. 18:21-35** carefully. Notice verses 33-35, " 'Shouldn't you have had mercy on your fellow servant just as I had on you?' In anger his master turned him over to the jailers to be tortured, until he should pay back all he owed. **This is how my heavenly Father will treat each of you unless you forgive your brother from your heart.**" Notice the condition!

Obviously, if the servant was in jail he could never, throughout all eternity, earn the money to pay the extremely large sum he owed. **His refusal to forgive another who begged him for forgiveness negated his own sin-debt that was once cancelled! UNFORGIVENESS IS A VERY SUBTLE AND DANGEROUS SATANIC TEMPTATION, SINCE ALL OF US HAVE BEEN SINNED AGAINST!**

Gal. 5:15 reads, "If you keep on biting and devouring each other, watch out or you will be **destroyed by each other**." Unforgiveness, hatred and bitterness seem to be implied here, as are other works of the sinful nature.

XIII. The Weak Christian of 1 Cor. 8

1 Cor. 8:10,11 read, "For if anyone with a weak conscience sees you who have this knowledge eating in an idol's temple, won't he be emboldened to eat what has been sacrificed to idols? So this weak brother, for whom Christ died, is **destroyed** by your knowledge." The same Greek word rendered "destroyed" here is found in Jn. 3:16 and translated "perish" and also in Lk. 15:24 and translated "lost."

XIV. The Recent Convert Who Is Potentially a Spiritual Leader

2 Tim. 3 cites numerous conditions for a possible overseer. In

verse 6, we read: "**He must not be a recent convert, or he may become conceited and fall under the same judgment as the devil.**" Please note that the sin of pride in the heart of a Christian can lead to his spiritual death. Compare to Mk. 7:22,23. Also, there can be no question that Paul knew this possibility existed and taught others to take it seriously! Furthermore, it is clear from the Scriptures that the judgment or condemnation of the devil is **ETERNAL FIRE**. Matt. 25:41 reads, "Then he will say to those on his left, 'Depart from me, you who are cursed, into the **ETERNAL FIRE PREPARED FOR THE DEVIL AND HIS ANGELS.**' " Also, Rev. 20:10 states that the devil will finally end up in the lake of fire and be **tormented forever there**! Again we see, Paul was NOT a U. E. S. proponent to write of this possibility!

These fourteen examples refute what another U. E. S. proponent, James Montgomery Boice, openly said across national radio in doubt to the possibility of one losing their salvation:

> "*...Suppose it were possible to lose our salvation; suppose we could do something where we actually throw it away. Isn't it the case, we being as depraved as we are, apart from the grace of God that* ***not only would some lose it, we'd all lose it***" [21] (emphasis ours).

Also, these examples just listed and the David explanation, as cited earlier, refute the subtle, moderate strand of U. E. S., that is, a real Christian could never, after the point of salvation, practice blatant sin or die spiritually for any reason.

1 JOHN 2:19 EXPLAINED

With these fourteen examples in mind, one should interpret 1 Jn. 2:19, "They went out from us, but they did not really belong to us. For if they had belonged to us, they would have remained with us; but their going showed that none of them belonged to us." John can't be saying here that a saved person could never turn away from God, for there are numerous clear passages which teach otherwise, such as the ones you just read. (This is what this verse IS NOT SAYING; shortly we'll look at the immediate context to see what it IS SAYING.)

The U. E. S. proponent, who emphasizes 1 Jn. 2:19, is in error if he believes that one can't really be sure another is anything more than just a professing Christian, since only God can see the heart! The U. E. S. conclusion of this is part true and part false. (In the natural, we can't see the roots of a fruit tree, but we can examine the fruit to determine how healthy the unseen roots are!) Scripturally, while it is true that only God can see the heart, **Barnabas saw clear, observable evidence that "the grace of God" brought salvation to some at Antioch** (Acts 11:23)! Some of the evidences found in Scripture for such are: **THE WORLD HATING YOU (Jn. 15:19), and THINKING YOUR SEPARATION FROM THEIR BEHAVIOR IS STRANGE TO THE POINT WHERE THEY HEAP ABUSE ON YOU (1 Pet. 4:4). Also, true conversion to Christ means being "ASHAMED" OF YOUR PAST LIFE OF SIN (Rom. 6:21) and PROVING YOUR REPENTANCE BY YOUR DEEDS (Acts 26:20).** Certainly, these and other factors, like risking his life for the name of Jesus (Acts 15:26), caused the early church to rightly conclude Paul was definitely saved, even though he once hated Christians and tried to destroy the church through persecution. Also, Paul knew Timothy and Titus were definitely saved (2 Tim. 1:9; Tit. 3:5). He also believed "loyal yokefellow" could identify those whose names are in the book of life (Phil. 4:3)! Perhaps the clearest proof of salvation is Jn. 8:36: "**So if the Son sets you FREE, you will be FREE indeed.**" The context bears out Jesus is speaking of **freedom from slavery to sin**, v. 34. This is exactly what happened at Corinth. Before their salvation, some in this Greek city **WERE** sexually immoral, idolaters, adulterers, homosexuals, thieves, greedy, drunkards, slanderers and swindlers. This is clearly borne out in 1 Cor. 6:11: "And this is what some of you **WERE**. But you **WERE** washed, you **WERE** sanctified, you **WERE** justified in the name of the Lord Jesus and by the Spirit of our God." Because of the grace of God touching their lives, there was a clear, clean break from this type of behavior! **This also explains what it does NOT mean to be a "carnal Christian" (1 Cor. 3:3, K. J. V.). Clearly, from 1 Cor. 6:11, carnal Christianity doesn't allow for the types of sins cited in the two preceding verses that will exclude ANYONE from the kingdom of God.**

To learn what this extremely important verse (1 Jn. 2:19) in our controversy IS SAYING, we must closely examine: (1) the immediate context (1 Jn. 2:18-29) and (2) interpret this Scripture with other relevant Scripture, which has just been done.

The immediate context shows that false teachers (Gnostics), whom John calls "antichrist" (v.18) were teaching the group of Christians to whom John was writing: JESUS IS NOT THE

CHRIST (v.22). John wrote that such teachers were trying to "deceive" them (v.26) into believing their lie about the Lord's identity. John expresses his godly concern regarding the truth of Jesus Christ's identity remaining in these Christians, so **that they in turn will continue to remain in Christ and in the Father** (v.24).

The apostles [and prophets] are the "foundation" on which the church is built (Eph. 2:20). Furthermore, the early church "devoted themselves to **the apostles' teaching**" (Acts 2:42). The false teachers that John labeled "antichrist" apparently knew these things and were claiming to be apostles of Christ too, for the sake of more influence on the people. [Paul also battled with false apostles, 2 Cor. 11:13.] This is how the pronouns "they" and "them" in 1 Jn. 2:19 should be understood. In other words, we should interpret 1 Jn. 2:19 as follows: "They [false apostles] went out from us [true apostles - teaching others as they went], but they [false apostles] did not really belong to us [true apostles]. For if they [false apostles] had belonged to us [true apostles], they [false apostles] would have remained with us [that is, remained teaching the simple truth which they denied about Jesus being the Christ]; but their going [to teach their lies] showed that none of them [false apostles] belonged to us [true apostles, which they claimed to be and who know and teach the truth about Jesus]." Please note the immediate context shows that the ones that "went out from us" in v.19 **were false TEACHERS**, and not just ordinary laymen, as we would call them in our day!

In conclusion, we know the following: (1) If the U. E. S. interpretation of 1 Jn. 2:19 was correct, then we could **NEVER** know if someone was REALLY saved or just a professing Christian, who might NOT be saved. This position has already been dealt with and refuted with Scripture! (2) If the U. E. S. interpretation of this key verse is correct, then how could there be at least fourteen clear, Biblical examples of people and types of people who did indeed experience genuine salvation, then afterwards turned away from Christ to the point where they experienced spiritual death, as already cited? This too would be an impossibility! Therefore, by allowing the immediate context of 1 Jn. 2:19 and these other Scriptures to interpret this Scripture in question, we must reject the U. E. S. view of it.

4

⁎ The Book of Hebrews ⁎

The writer of Hebrews clearly wrote to Christians (3:1; 12:5,6), who were still infant and who were consequently rebuked for not growing (5:11-14). They also had spiritually "feeble arms and weak knees" (12:12) and forgot certain encouraging truths (12:5). In the beginning of their spiritual walk, the gospel was preached to them (4:2), they received the spiritual light from it (10:32) and stood their ground even after they were subjected to various painful forms of persecution, which included public insults and the confiscation of their property which they joyfully accepted (10:32-34). Implied was their giving up assembling together (10:25) and neglecting in a general way their great salvation (2:3). Now it was necessary to exhort [caution strongly] them (13:22), which indeed is done over and over again in this book. Note the warnings that were issued to these feeble and infant Christians who were not growing spiritually. Please ponder them carefully:

- "We must pay more careful attention, therefore, to what we have heard, so that we do not drift away. For if the message spoken by angels was binding, and every violation and disobedience received its just punishment, how shall we escape if we ignore such a great salvation?...." (2:1-3).

- "But Christ is faithful as a son over God's house. And we are his house, **IF** we hold on to our courage and the hope of which we boast" (3:6).

- **"See to it, brothers, that none of you has a sinful, unbelieving heart that TURNS AWAY from the living God. But encourage one another daily, as long as it is called Today, so that none of you may be hardened by sin's deceitfulness. WE HAVE COME TO SHARE IN CHRIST <u>IF</u> WE HOLD FIRMLY <u>TILL THE END</u> THE CONFIDENCE WE HAD AT FIRST"** (3:12-14).

- "Therefore, since the promise of entering his rest still stands, let us be careful that none of you be found to have fallen short of it" (4:1).

- "Let us, therefore, make every effort to enter that rest, so that no one will fall by following their example of disobedience" (4:11).

- "...let us hold firmly to the faith we profess" (4:14b).

- "It is impossible for those who have once been enlightened, who have tasted the heavenly gift, who have shared in the Holy Spirit, who have tasted the goodness of the word of God and the powers of the coming age, IF they fall away to be brought back to repentance, because to their loss they are crucifying the Son of God all over again and subjecting him to public disgrace. Land that drinks in the rain often falling on it and that produces a crop useful to those for whom it is farmed receives the blessing of God. But land that produces thorns and thistles is worthless and is **in danger of being cursed. In the end it will be burned**. Even though we speak like this, dear friends, we are confident of better things in your case - things that accompany salvation" (6:4-9).

[**COMMENT**: How some reduce Heb. 6:4-6 to refer to a sinner under conviction is shocking! Furthermore, such can only be possible because of preconceived doctrinal biases and/or a refusal to see the plain and obvious!]

- "We want each of you to **show this same diligence to the very end, in order to make your hope sure**. We do not want you to become lazy, but to imitate those who through faith and patience inherit what has been promised" (6:11,12).

- "Let us not give up meeting together, as some are in the habit of doing, but let us encourage one another - and all the more as you see the Day approaching" (10:25).

- "If we deliberately keep on sinning **after we have received the knowledge of the truth**, no sacrifice for sins is left, but only a fearful expectation of judgment and of **RAGING FIRE THAT WILL CONSUME THE ENEMIES OF GOD**. Anyone who rejected the law of Moses died without mercy on the testimony of two or three witnesses. How much more severely do you think a man deserves to be punished who has trampled the Son of God under foot, who has treated as an unholy thing the blood of the covenant **that sanctified him**, and who has insulted the Spirit of grace? For we know him who said, 'It is mine to avenge; I will repay,' and again, 'The Lord will judge his people.' It is a dreadful thing to fall into the hands of the living God" (10:26-31).

- "So do not throw away your confidence; it will be richly rewarded. **You need to persevere so that when you have done the will of God, you will receive what he has promised.** For in just a very little while, 'He who is coming will come and will not delay. But my righteous one will live by faith. And **if he shrinks back, I will not be pleased with him.' But we are not of those who SHRINK BACK AND ARE DESTROYED, but of those who believe and are saved" (10:35-39).**

- "Consider him who endured such opposition from sinful men, so that you will not grow weary and lose heart" (12:3).

- "See that no one is sexually immoral, or is godless like Esau, who for a single meal sold his inheritance rights as the oldest son. Afterward, as you know, when he wanted to inherit this blessing, he was rejected. He could bring about no change of mind, though he sought the blessing with tears" (12:16,17).

- "See to it that you do not refuse him who speaks. If they did not escape when they refused him who warned them on earth, how much less will we, **if we turn away from him** who **WARNS** us from heaven? At that time his voice shook the earth, but now he has promised, 'Once more I will shake not only the earth but also the heavens.' The words 'once more' indicate the removing of what can be shaken - that is, created things - so that what cannot be shaken may remain" (12:25-27).

WHAT ABOUT HEBREWS 6:4-6?

Because Heb. 6:4-6 has long been a passage of controversy in itself, a comment is needed regarding it. Unfortunately, some refer to this passage to try to prove that a person can only get saved once, and if he turns to follow Satan for a time afterwards, he can NEVER come back to God and get saved again! This has caused incredible emotional pain in the lives of those who have accepted this as a Biblical truth, then have turned from God for a time and would like to come back, but think that they can't, based on this passage!

Before we focus in upon Peter, to learn more about this passage, let's notice that **Heb. 6:4-6 cites five spiritual checkpoints that one must experience before these verses can even be a consideration in their own life!** After examining the Apostle Peter, his "fall" and subsequent return to the Lord, some will be quite surprised and very relieved to learn that **VERY FEW** ever reach the level of spiritual maturity in Christ that is spoken of in these verses! These verses should absolutely **NOT** be understood like D. James Kennedy wrote about them, placing no stipulation upon one's spiritual maturity to make his position more credible:

> "*This destroys the idea that we may be saved and lost and saved and lost, for it says that it is impossible if we should fall away to renew us again unto repentance. It is impossible. If you are saved and you are lost, if that is what this means, then you have had one shot at it, my friends and you have blown it! You're through! It is impossible to renew you again unto repentance. So it's only one time at bat.*" [22]

Again, only certain few Christians are being referred to in Heb. 6:4-6 as evident by the five spiritual checkpoints and the following facts about Peter.

Though we can't be certain, it appears Peter walked with Jesus for about three years during the Lord's earthly ministry. During those unique years Peter experienced the following: He had the unique privilege of being at the Mt. of Transfiguration where Moses and Elijah appeared and talked with Jesus. He, at this time, also heard the audible voice of God say, "This is my Son, whom I love; with him I am well pleased. Listen to him" (Matt. 17:1-6)! Peter was the ONLY apostle of the Twelve to actually walk on the water for a time with Jesus (Matt. 14:29)! He was given powerful spiritual authority to drive out demons and heal **every** disease and sickness (Matt. 10:1). The Apostle Peter personally saw Jesus raise three different people from the dead (Lk. 7:14,15; 8:54,55 and Jn. 11:43,44)! He also saw Jesus' power instantly heal a leper (Matt. 8:2,3), enable a paralytic to be healed (Matt. 9:2-7), the blind to see (Mk. 8:22-25), and the dumb to speak after a demon was driven out (Matt. 9:32,33). In fact, Peter was there when at least 2,000 demons inside a man were BEG-

GING Jesus for permission to go inside pigs, when He cast them out (Mk. 5:12,13). He witnessed Jesus calm the wind and the raging sea with His word (Mk. 4:39). For years, Peter heard the GREATEST AND WISEST teacher that ever lived teach the most important truths with authority. He also had unique and vital spiritual truth revealed to him about Jesus directly from the Father (Matt. 16:16,17). Peter heard the demons within people call Jesus the "Son of God" (Mk. 3:11). He heard Jesus silence those who tried to trap Him (Lk. 20:20-26), perfectly answer and handle every trick question (Matt. 22:23-31) and remedy every problem that confronted them (Matt. 17:27; etc.). Peter saw Jesus multiply bread and fish to feed thousands of people on two different occasions (Matt. 16:9,10). After all this, he denied Christ three

THE APOSTLE PETER WAS NOT SO MATURE SPIRITUALLY THAT HE COULD NOT RETURN TO JESUS.

times! YET, THE APOSTLE PETER WAS NOT SO MATURE SPIRITUALLY THAT HE COULD NOT RETURN TO JESUS, **EVEN CONSIDERING HEB. 6:4-6**!

There is little chance that you, the reader, have ever known any Christian on a par with Peter before his "fall"! Therefore, Heb. 6:4-6 would apply to such **few** people that the vast majority of Christians don't even come close to qualifying because of the five awesome conditions cited in that passage, which **even the Apostle Peter didn't meet!** (Remember also Lk. 15:24,32 and Rom. 11:23 which state that **one can be saved more than once**.)

Finally, after Peter's thrice denial of Jesus, he was the one used on the day of Pentecost, about 50 days later, to win thousands to Christ! He also had the distinguished honor of writing two of the twenty-seven New Testament books! In fact, after the Apostle Paul, Peter (who once "fell away") won more people to the Lord than any other Christian, according to the New Testament record!

WHAT ABOUT HEBREWS 10:26-31?

This passage has also caused much confusion and grief over the years regarding its true meaning. Perhaps Myer Pearlman can illuminate its true meaning for you as he briefly touches on Heb.

6:4-6:

> *"Those addressed were* ***Hebrew Christians****, who, discouraged and persecuted, (10:32-39)* ***were tempted to return to Judaism. Before being received again into the synagogue*** *they would be publicly required to make the following statements (10:29): that Jesus was not the Son of God; that His blood was rightly shed as that of a common malefactor; and that His miracles were done by the power of the evil one. All this is implied in 10:29. (That such a repudiation would have been insisted on is illustrated by the case of a Hebrew Christian in Germany, who desired to return to the synagogue, but was refused when he desired to hold on to some of the New Testament truths.) Before their conversion they had belonged to the nation which had crucified Christ;* ***to return to the synagogue*** *would be to crucify to themselves the Son of God afresh and put Him to an open shame; it would be the awful sin of apostasy (Heb. 6:6); it would be like the unpardonable sin for which there is no forgiveness, because the one so hardened as to commit it cannot be 'renewed unto repentance'; it would be worthy of a worse punishment than that of death (10:28); it would mean incurring the vengeance of the living God. 10:30,31"* [23] (emphasis ours).

5

* Paul's "Freedom" (or "Liberty") Message for Christians *

As mentioned earlier, Christian "freedom" or "liberty" (K.J.V.) does exist! This is clear from Gal. 2:4 and 5:1. However, as we shall soon see, it's not the kind of freedom that allows for, or even tolerates, unholy or immoral behavior. Much confusion exists regarding this subject in our day. A prime example is what a U. E. S. proponent told me years ago in response to what I personally observed on TV - a "minister" who was wearing a cowboy hat and smoking a cigar as he mockingly sang the gospel song, Amazing Grace. The U. E. S. proponent said to me, *"He's abusing his Christian liberty."* How desperately we need to know the truth on this topic, as evident from **some being unable to distinguish blasphemy from Christian liberty abuse!**

Repeatedly, we who are Christians are commanded to "**be holy,**" that is, in our **BEHAVIOR** (1 Thess. 4:3-7; 2 Tim. 1:9; 1 Pet. 1:15,16; 2 Pet. 3:11), even after we have already been declared "holy" and "sanctified" in Christ at the point of salvation (Acts 26:18; 1 Cor. 1:2,30)! **Since Scripture doesn't contradict Scripture, we know that our FREEDOM in Christ, therefore, can NOT interfere with this repeated command!** To say otherwise is to show yourself deceived! Holy living is not optional for the Christian in spite of his allowed liberties! **It is still a COMMAND for us, as it was in the Old Testament, as Peter points out (1 Pet. 1:15,16 cf. Lev. 11:44; 19:2).**

Paul's freedom in Christ message, as mentioned in Gal. 2:4 and 5:1, refers to freedom from practicing **circumcision** (5:1-4), and **observing special Jewish days, months, seasons and years** (4:10), which would include keeping the Sabbaths, Passover, Pentecost, Tabernacles, and the sabbatical year. See also Col. 2:16,17.

Furthermore, Paul's teaching in Rom. 14 shows that **we are not under any "unclean" food regulations**, as set forth in Lev. 11. [This allows us the freedom to eat shrimp, crabs, lobster and pork, if we so desire! However, we are still forbidden to eat or drink blood (Acts 15:20,29) as in the Old Testament days (Lev. 7:26, 27)!] Similarly, according to 1 Cor. 8, Paul allowed the Corinthian Christians to eat meat sacrificed to an idol; but added that this "**freedom**" could become a stumbling block to the Christian that didn't have this knowledge and possibly might be "destroyed" by such an example. Therefore, he advised them to surrender this freedom for the sake of others, vv. 9-13! **In other words, it was "freedom" regarding the eating of food, WITH RESTRICTIONS ATTACHED!**

"YOU, MY BROTHERS, WERE CALLED TO BE FREE. BUT DO NOT USE YOUR FREEDOM TO INDULGE THE SINFUL NATURE."

Perhaps the clearest single verse of Scripture which refutes the present-day, counterfeit "freedom" or "liberty" in Christ message is found in Gal. 5:13: "**You, my brothers, were called to be free. But do NOT use your freedom to indulge the sinful nature.**" This is what Paul, the grace teacher, wrote about our Christian freedom in Christ! Finally, it is in this same epistle to the Galatians, which **EMPHASIZES CHRISTIAN LIBERTY,** that Paul wrote his often-repeated **WARNING to Christians**: "The acts of the sinful nature are obvious: sexual immorality, impurity and debauchery; idolatry and witchcraft; hatred, discord, jealousy, fits of rage, selfish ambition, dissensions, factions and envy; drunkenness, orgies, and the like. **I WARN YOU, AS I DID BEFORE, that those who live like this will NOT inherit the kingdom of God**" (5:19-21).

[Peter likewise taught: "**Live as free men, but DO NOT USE YOUR FREEDOM AS A COVER-UP FOR EVIL; LIVE AS SERVANTS OF GOD,**" 1 Pet. 2:16! Implied in this verse is the distortion of Scripture regarding our "freedom" in Christ by some to "**cover-up evil**"! (Could this be the reason why the distorted liberty message of our day is so popular, that is, to cover up evil behavior?) Apparently, this was a problem in Peter's day, **as it is today**! Regarding this, Peter speaks of certain false teachers:

"They promise them **freedom**, while they themselves are slaves of depravity - for a man is a slave to whatever has mastered him" (2 Pet. 2:19).

"LIVE AS FREE MEN, BUT DO NOT USE YOUR FREEDOM AS A COVER-UP FOR EVIL; LIVE AS SERVANTS OF GOD."

Though Paul was "not under the law" (1 Cor. 9:20), he was "under Christ's law" (1 Cor. 9:21)! Christ's law seems best described in Gal. 6:2: "Carry each other's burdens, and in this way you will fulfill the law of Christ."

Furthermore, while Paul taught Christians: "We are not under law but under grace" (Rom. 6:15); the rest of the same passage on down to verse 22 declares: (1) Sin "leads to death" while obedience "leads to righteousness," v.16. (2) Offer the parts of your body in **"slavery to righteousness leading to holiness,"** v.19. (3) **THE RESULT OF HOLINESS IS ETERNAL LIFE (v.22)!** THESE TRUTHS SHOULD NOT BE EXCLUDED FROM PAUL'S GRACE MESSAGE. TO DO SO CAN EASILY MISREPRESENT IT!

Paul could say, "We are not under the law," yet it is a Scriptural fact that he (and other inspired New Testament writers) taught Christians **AGAINST** the following: FALSE GODS (1 Cor. 8:4-6); MAKING GRAVEN IMAGES (Acts 19:26); and expanded IDOLATRY to include GREED (Eph. 5:5; Col. 3:5), which is another term for COVETING; THE MISUSE OF GOD'S NAME and PROFANITY (Eph. 5:4; Col. 3:8); MURDER (Rev. 21:8) and expanded its meaning to include HATRED OF A BROTHER (1 Jn. 3:15); ADULTERY or SEXUAL IMMORALITY (1 Cor. 6:9,10; Gal. 5:19-21); STEALING (Eph. 4:28; Tit. 2:10); BEARING FALSE WITNESS or SLANDER and LYING (1 Cor. 6:9,10; Eph. 4:25,31; Col. 3:8,9; Tit. 3:2). He also was **FOR** HONORING ONE'S FATHER AND MOTHER (Eph. 6:1-3), just like the Ten Commandments (Ex. 20:1-17; Deut. 5:6-21)! **Eph. 6:1-3 is MOST CLEAR on this point!** In conclusion, Paul taught we are **NOT** UNDER THE CEREMONIAL LAW AS EVIDENT FROM GALATIANS, but we as Christians are under Christ's law even though we are **"under grace" and "saved by grace"!** Though he, at times, stressed that, "The entire law is summed up in a single command: 'Love your neighbor as yourself' " (Gal. 5:14 cf. Rom. 13:8-10); **Paul also stressed the behavior or moral aspects of the Christian life too**, as just cited! Therefore, legalism in the New Testament is connected with the ceremonial law and **NOT** the obeying of the moral commands! In other words, **we as Christians today, though not "under the law," are NOT permitted to steal, get drunk, and/or be sexually immoral.** To do so is to show you do not love Jesus (Jn. 14:24), besides revealing your dead spiritual condition (1 Cor. 6:9,10).

[Regarding the Sabbath command **NOT** being in effect today, Deut. 5:15 shows WHY and to WHOM the Sabbath command was given. In other words, it was set up specifically for THE JEWS to remember their historical deliverance from bitter slavery in the country of Egypt. Therefore, the Sabbath command was set up in a similar way as the Passover - a yearly memorial festival for the Jews to celebrate in memory of God, who passed over the houses of the Israelites in Egypt because of the blood, while the firstborn of the Egyptians were struck dead (Ex. 12:14-30).]

Sometimes connected with the freedom in Christ message is Rom. 7:15-20. Some have erroneously alluded to this passage to justify worldly living and carnal behavior. Remember this, we should **ALWAYS compare Scripture with Scripture when studying the Bible.** If this is done, it will become apparent that Paul didn't "keep on doing" sinful things, as he frequently taught against! Please consider what he wrote about himself elsewhere: "He [Timothy] will remind you of **my way of life in Christ Jesus, which agrees with what I teach everywhere in every church**" (1 Cor. 4:17). Also, he wrote: "**Whatever you** have learned or received or **heard from me, or seen in me - put it into practice. And the God of peace will be with you**" (Phil. 4:9). Moreover, he declared: "You are witnesses, and so is God, of how **holy, righteous and blameless we were among you who believed**" (1 Thess. 2:10). Finally, how could Paul have stated, "I have fought the good fight, I have finished the race, I have kept the faith" (2 Tim. 4:7) at the very end of his life, if he was habitually worldly and blatantly disobedient like many today who passively profess to be Christians? Since the Christian battle, in part, is against sin (Heb. 12:4), Paul fought this fight against sin also in his own life and came out as an overcomer.

The Christian is "free," but at the same time, he is "**Christ's slave**" (1 Cor. 7:22) and a "**slave to righteousness**" (Rom. 6:18)! As freed people, we are to be living for Jesus and His cause (2

Cor. 5:15). In fact, service to God is an immediate responsibility after turning from our idols that kept us in spiritual darkness and death (1 Thess. 1:9 cf. Jonah 2:8). With these verses in mind, how could the real freedom in Christ message, coupled with the true grace message, which teaches us to live godly lives (Tit. 2:12), overlook lukewarm, worldly, entertainment-seeking, amusement-seeking, pleasure-seeking "servants" who have very little or no fear of God?

"AND HIS COMMANDS ARE NOT BURDENSOME."

In contrast to what some think and have been taught, living a holy life is NOT burdensome. Jesus said, "For **my yoke is EASY** and **my burden is LIGHT**" (Matt. 11:30). John wrote, "**And his commands are NOT BURDENSOME**" (1 Jn. 5:3b). See also Psa. 19:7-11; 119:14. The opposite, however, is true for the ungodly, that is, living an unholy and rebellious lifestyle is BURDENSOME. Jeremiah 2:19 says, " 'Your wickedness will **punish** you; your backsliding will **rebuke** you. Consider then and realize how evil and **bitter** it is for you when you forsake the Lord your God and have no awe of me,' declares the Lord, the LORD Almighty." Furthermore, regarding drunkenness specifically, we read, "Who has **woe**? Who has **sorrow**? Who has **strife**? Who has **complaints**? Who has **needless bruises**? Who has **bloodshot eyes**? Those who linger over wine, who go to sample bowls of mixed wine...Your eyes will **see strange sights** and your mind **imagine confusing things**. You will be **like one sleeping on the high seas, lying on top of the rigging**. 'They hit me,' you will say, 'but I'm not hurt! They beat me, but **I don't feel it**! When will I wake up so I can find another drink?' " (Prov. 23:29,30,33-35). Finally, the bondage, burden and slavery to sin is graphically expressed in the following: "**The evil deeds of a wicked man ENSNARE him; THE CORDS OF HIS SIN HOLD HIM FAST**" (Prov. 5:22). This is what the FREEDOM mentioned in Jn. 8:36 is all about, that is, FREEDOM from sin's bondages: "So if the Son sets you free, you will be free indeed."

Heb. 4 speaks of a "sabbath rest" for the people of God. It should be very clear at this point in the book that it is **IMPOSSIBLE** for this "sabbath rest" to mean that one can be close to God and be carefree and indifferent to his Christian responsibilities, duties, and obligations as a servant living under grace.

Finally, Paul wrote twice, "Everything is permissible for me - but not everything is beneficial" (1 Cor. 6:12; 10:23). The context of both verses is primarily referring to the eating of food. Again, **the correct interpretation of these verses will not contradict holy behavior for the Christian!**

A prime example of this kind of distortion is the following answer given by Bob George on nationwide radio:

> **CALLER**: "*Can a child of God use it, use the marijuana?*" **GEORGE**: "*Can a child of, what, God [sic] can do anything they [sic] want to, 'everything is permissible but not everything is profitable' but to deny [sic] the problem isn't in his usage of marijuana. The problem is in his denial of the truth.*" (A little later in the same program), **GEORGE:** "*...so I could, **as far as a child of God is concerned, I COULD GO OUT AS A CHILD OF GOD AND GET DRUNK TONIGHT IF I WANTED TO. It's not that, if, if, if it, if it [sic] was not permissible**, then it would be a law, **but it's not profitable***" [24] (emphasis ours).

George said a similar appalling thing in a more clear way on a different radio broadcast:

> "*And as Paul said, 'All things are permissible, but not all things are profitable.' **SO IS COMMITTING FORNICATION PERMISSIBLE? YES.** Is it profitable? No, it isn't*" [25] (emphasis ours).

To whom did he speak these words directly? A young man from New York who has been having a **habitual problem with sexual sin**!

[Reader, if you conduct yourself according to what you just read (as it is being taught all across the United States by way of radio as being "*permissible*"), **YOU WILL GO TO HELL**, according to Scripture! Do not be deceived, the wicked will not inherit the kingdom of God (1 Cor. 6:9). The truth is: we are to "**abstain**" from (Acts 15:20,29), "**flee**" from (1 Cor. 6:18), and "**avoid**" sexual immorality (1 Thess. 4:3).]

"TOLERATING JEZEBEL"

What do you think Jesus would say to us today about this type of reprehensible teaching and those who tolerate it? In Rev. 2:20-22, the Lord Jesus, now resurrected and ascended into Heaven, said, "...I have this against you: You **tolerate** that woman Jezebel...by her teaching she misleads my servants into sexual immorality...." Please note the following: **To "tolerate" teachings that lead Christians into sin, especially sexual immorality, is condemned in itself by the Lord!** The word "tolerate" is defined as: *To allow to be or be done* ***without active opposition***. In other words, to be stirred for the moment without doing anything to help correct this serious problem is to "tolerate Jezebel," which allows this evil to spread.

> **TOLERATE - to allow to be or be done <u>without active opposition</u>.**

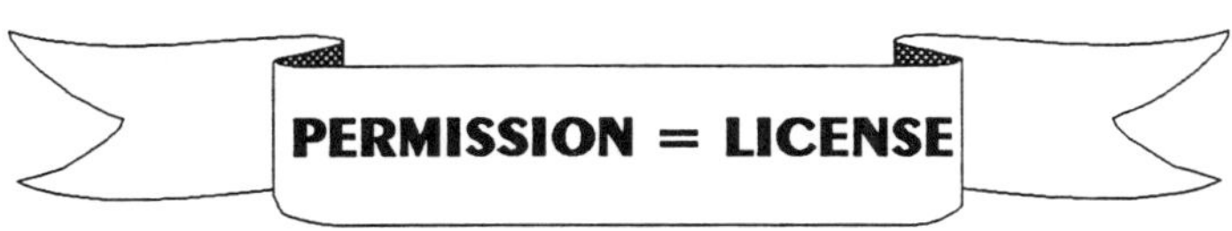

Finally, Jude 4 speaks of those who "change the grace of God into a **license** for immorality." **Since "license" and "permission" are synonyms, that is, they have the same meaning - to say drunkenness and/or fornication is "*permissible*" for the Christian is to give "license" for immorality through a perverted grace message!** This is what the Jude 3 command, "contend for the faith" was given to counter!

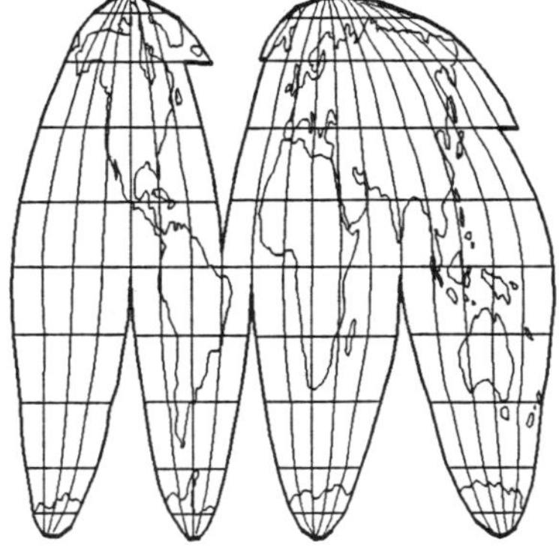

In light of all this, it is ironic that CRI, an international countercult ministry, which frequently mentions the "contend for the faith" command of Jude

3, could give the following coast to coast endorsement of Bob George over their radio program, The Bible Answer Man (1/3/94) via Dr. Ron Rhodes:

> *"I understand where Bob George is coming from on that. I've got to tell you, however, that we at CRI disagree with his interpretation, especially in terms of 1 John 1:9.* ***Now we believe that Bob George, in the big picture, is A GREAT BROTHER. He has done A LOT OF GOOD THINGS FOR THE CHRISTIAN COMMUNITY. So in the big picture, we consider himself [sic] A FRIEND OF THE MINISTRY,*** *but the small picture is, is [sic] that in 1 John 1 verse 9 that talks about our confessing sins, we believe that that is something that the Christian is to do..."* (emphasis ours).

[QUESTIONS FOR DR. RON: Do you consider such teachings that permit drunkenness and/or fornication for the Christian to be a "*good thing for the Christian community*"? Do you think Jude would consider Bob George "*a friend*" of his ministry, in light of Jude 3,4? THANK YOU for openly disagreeing with his unscriptural view of 1 Jn. 1:9, but why did you neglect to mention this other extremely unscriptural view of his?]

Could it be that unwittingly, Rhodes and others like him who approve such teachings by endorsing the teacher/s in the "*big picture*" are sharing in their "wicked work" (2 Jn. 11)?

6

* By George, What A Grace Message! *

The radio talk show, People to People, aired from Dallas, Texas with host Bob George, broadcasted the following on September 29, 1993. Since this radio show can be heard across the United States, certainly untold tens of thousands were listening to this staunch U. E. S. proponent verbalizing his distorted views of the grace message with his easy-to-listen-to voice and friendly personality. **HOW MANY, DO YOU THINK, FROM YOUR CONGREGATION WERE LISTENING TO THIS BROADCAST AND WERE ADVERSELY AFFECTED?** (Bold print is used to emphasize certain points from that broadcast.)

*"...And it also talks about, that we have an inheritance that is guaranteed and of course, **a guarantee is only valid if the guarantor is, is [sic] responsible. And our guarantor is Christ Jesus.** It says he is the guarantor of the covenant that we are under today, so we have a guarantor that first of all, if we believe he's who he said he is, and that's God, then we don't have to wonder whether he meant what he said or not when he said I guarantee that you have an eternal inheritance and I guarantee that you have a life that is called eternal life. Now why we doubt that, I don't know, but at any rate, **I believe it's because we doubt our guarantor. In the final analysis, that's what it amounts to, is our guarantor is flimsy, and therefore, we cannot have confidence in the guarantee.**"*

*"...The Jesus of the Bible is the one who said, 'I will never leave you nor forsake you.' Now, if you're inviting Jesus, who you think is going to leave you or forsake you into your heart, when Jesus said 'I'll never leave you or forsake you,' **you've got another Jesus** you've invited in there, because **that's not the one in the Bible.** The Jesus of the Bible is the one who said I will never, ever, ever leave you nor forsake you. That Jesus is the one in the Bible."*

"...***Backsliding doesn't come from sin, it comes from the sin, and that is the sin of unbelief in the denial of the grace of God that covered your sin. In other words, the way that you fall away from God is not through sinning because you're never going to stop your flesh.*** *As long as you are living in this body of flesh, you are going to find that that body of flesh is always going to be raising up its ugly head. But if you walk in unbelief in regard to Christ's provision for that sin, that's what enables you, as the Bible says, that you are alienated from God in your own mind because of your evil behavior. It's in your mind, it's not in his. Christ has taken away your sin.* ***So the way people get away, Jeff, from, from, from [sic], Christ is not through the alleviation of sinning.*** *There isn't anybody who's going to stop that, or can stop that as long as we're in the flesh.* ***But we get away from Christ when we forget, when we forget [sic] his provision for that....You're not on any road toward perfection, you've already been made perfect in the sight of God.*** *Let me give you an example of that, Jeff, so that you don't live in deception on that....* ***There's no sin that can take you on to spiritual death,*** *you're already dead, you were born dead and when you came alive in Christ, you came alive eternally....Now that's what salvation is, is [sic] the receiving of life, and that's why the cross had to take away man's sin,* ***because had the cross not taken away man's sin, and you received life, the very next time you sinned, you'd die because the wages of sin is not backsliding, the wages of sin is not being out of fellowship, the wages of sin is not getting a paddling, the wages of sin is death.*** *So the only solution to death was life and it was a life called eternal life and that's why the cross is so important for us to understand the finality of it, is because if it wasn't for the cross, when we got life, we would just die the next time we sinned again. So it's the cross that gives you, that enables you to, to [sic] obtain a life called eternal life.* ***So, there is no sinning unto death, as a person who has been made alive, because there isn't anything to kill you. Sins that caused death are behind the back of God never to see it again.*** *So that's why a person, like you say, backslidden into death, that's an impossibility.* ***Now there, there [sic] are people who have never been saved and there are people who are saved who can certainly get involved in the, the, the [sic] flesh but it's never going to create death for them. What it creates, and again, the sin is, I can't get this across enough, the sin is not the issue, it's when you stop believing God's provision for that sin, is what alienates you from God. Your own sin, looked upon in truth, is 'Lord, that was a sin that I just did, but it's behind the back of God never to see it again. It was forgiven at the cross, Jesus did it all for me. Now, Lord, you living in me,*** *renew my mind and teach me truth that will set me free. In other words, what I want to know now, is how do I change my mind in regard to that.' "*

"...And what we have done is bring the context of 1 John 1:9 over to a believer instead of realizing it was a passage for salvation. It was a passage to a person denying that they had a sin nature....[I]t's a case of putting the verse where it belongs, either to a lost person or to a saved person. And if it's to a saved person, then you've negated everything that Christ did at the cross, because you're saying that God was in Christ reconciling the world unto himself, not counting your sins against you, and then turn around and saying, [sic] but if you confess, he'll forgive you, and that's double talk."

❧ ❧ ❧ ❧ ❧

(A Biblical Response To Bob George)

Yes, George is right that the Holy Spirit is a deposit guaranteeing our inheritance (Eph. 1:13,14), but to conclude "*There's no sin that can take you on to spiritual death*" is a contradiction of Paul's grace message, as clearly cited in Rom. 8:13; 1 Cor. 6:9,10; Gal. 5:19-21; 6:8! **PAUL REPEATEDLY WARNED CHRISTIANS** that living in certain sinful ways would definitely cause them to "**NOT inherit the kingdom of God**" (Gal. 5:21). Certainly, Paul was not inferring Jesus is "*flimsy*" or that one has "*another Jesus*" if he rejects the U. E. S. rationale as cited. Also, Paul and other apostles mention free will and human responsibility in their teachings, which seem to be the key missing elements in the teaching of the U. E. S. proponents. (See Col. 3:5-8; 1 Tim. 5:22; 1 Jn. 5:21; etc.) While George teaches "*You're never going to stop your flesh,*" or "*Backsliding doesn't come from sin,*" Paul, the real grace teacher, taught Christians: "**For if you live according to the sinful nature, you will die; but if by the Spirit YOU PUT TO DEATH the misdeeds of the body, you will live**" (Rom. 8:13)! [Paul believed we not only could, but better put our flesh (or sinful nature) to death.] He also taught Christians: "**The one who sows to please his sinful nature, from that nature will reap destruction**; the one who sows to please the Spirit, from the Spirit will reap eternal life" (Gal. 6:8). It's our choice to do either. If we make the right choice, then it's our responsibility, as we rely on God, to do it.

Furthermore, Paul commanded Christians to: "Aim for perfection" (2 Cor. 13:11) and also prayed for their "perfection" (2 Cor. 13:9). In contrast to Paul, George teaches "*You're not on any road to perfection, you've already been made perfect in the sight of God*" in his "grace" message! Paul wrote, "**Not that I** have already obtained all this, or **have already been made perfect**, but I press on to take hold of that for which Christ Jesus took hold of me" (Phil. 3:12).

While it's true that "The wages of sin is death" (Rom. 6:23), and not something else, the facts as laid out by James from temptation to spiritual death were not mentioned: "But each one is tempted when, by his own evil desire, he is dragged away and enticed. Then, after desire has conceived, it gives birth to sin; and **sin, when it is full-grown**, gives birth to **DEATH**" (Jam. 1:14,15). Furthermore, there are different degrees of sin (Mk. 3:29; Jn. 19:11; 1 Cor. 6:18; 1 Jn. 5:16,17)! Worry and unthankfulness are not in the same category as greed, sexual immorality, drunkenness and/or lying, which will send anyone to the lake of fire (1 Cor. 6:9,10; Rev. 21:8)! **While it's true that Rom. 14:23 says, "Everything that does not come from faith is sin," this, however, is NOT the all-encompassing definition for sin for the Christian, as set forth in the New Testament.** Elsewhere we learn: (1) "Anyone, then, who knows the good he ought to do and doesn't do it, **sins**," Jam. 4:17 and (2) "All wrongdoing is **sin**," 1 Jn. 5:17.

If 1 Jn. 1:9 applies only to the unbeliever or "*lost person,*" as broadcasted across the United States, then **how could an unbeliever remember all of his innumerable sins to confess them to be saved?** Furthermore, Lk. 18:13 shows an unsaved person not confessing his sins specifically by name, but instead, asking for mercy in a general way which brought instant justification! Acts 10:43-48 cf. 11:14 is also crystal clear in countering this application of 1 Jn. 1:9 for it shows **Cornelius and his household got saved without uttering a word, that is, without confessing a sin!** Since 1 Jn. 1:9, therefore, can NOT refer to the unbeliever getting saved, it must refer to the believer, that is, he/she getting certain sins forgiven AFTER their salvation! 1 Jn. 1:7 cites the possibility of receiving a continuous purifying from sin by the blood of Christ, **but only if we meet the cited condition of walking "in the light, as he is in the light."** Clearly this is written for the believer. Also, 1 Jn. 2:1 was clearly written for the believer. So we now have two clear references, just two verses before and two verses after 1 Jn. 1:9 written to the believer! Doesn't the flow of this group of verses refute George's usage of 1 Jn. 1:9 for the unbeliever? Finally, 1 Jn. 1:9 reads, "If **we** confess **our** sins, he is faithful and just and will forgive **us our** sins and purify **us** from all unrighteousness." Please note the plural pronouns in this verse. The Apostle John put himself in this group, which obviously refers to the believer AFTER initial salvation. He, therefore, could not have been trying to "*negate everything that Christ did at the cross*" nor was he guilty of "*double talk.*" Sin, therefore, must still be an "*issue*" as shown in this verse and all throughout the New Testament. Moreover, Psa. 51:1-12 cf. **Psa. 32:5** is clear that David, **AFTER his salvation**, confessed his sins to God after he committed adultery with Bathsheba, to get forgiven. Certainly, no one would argue he did it to receive forgiveness at the point of initial salvation. **Since 1 Jn. 1:9 is the God-given way of getting forgiven after salvation, not to confess our sins, therefore, means not to get forgiven!**

Rev. 21:5-8 is also very clear that it won't be just the unbelievers that go to the lake of fire! In fact, such aren't even mentioned first in this list that do!

Revelation chapters 2 and 3 are also very clear in showing that sin is indeed the "*issue*" with the risen Lord and His children; especially note chapter 2 verses 20-24. Paul also made sin the

"Dear children, do not let anyone lead you astray. He who does what is right is righteous, just as he is righteous. He who does what is sinful is of the devil..." (1 Jn. 3:7,8).

issue in his teachings (1 Cor. 6:9,10; Gal. 5:19-21; 6:8; Eph. 5:5-7; Col. 3:5-8; 1 Thess. 4:3-8; etc.) as does the Apostle John in 1 Jn. 1:7-2:1; 3:7,8. **Finally, note what the Lord Jesus said about SIN BEING THE ISSUE in Matt. 13:40-42 and Mk. 9:42-48.** To discount this because he said this BEFORE the cross is to discount virtually all of his teachings, including: Jesus is the only way to the Father (Jn. 14:6), one must be "born again" to enter the kingdom of God (Jn. 3:5), and unless one repents, he will perish (Lk. 13:3). All these truths were also taught AFTER the cross by the disciples. **In conclusion, to teach "*sin is not the issue*" is not only erroneous but spiritually dangerous, since it undermines the potential danger latent within sin!** Remember, false teachers in first-century Christianity and in our day have the ability of changing the grace message "into a license for immorality" (Jude 4)!

7

✲ U. E. S. Arguments and Proof Texts ✲

This refutation to U. E. S. would be incomplete if the primary proof texts and objections offered by the U. E. S. proponents were not dealt with and explained from Scripture. The following are additional objections that were not yet dealt with in this controversy. (Already explained were Jn. 6:64; Rom. 8:35-39; 2 Tim. 2:13 and 1 Jn. 2:19. Therefore, they will not be dealt with here.)

OBJECTION #1. Jesus said, "I give them eternal life, and they shall never perish, no one can snatch them out of my hand," Jn. 10:28. Therefore, if, having received eternal life, we could lose it and perish, it would make Christ a liar.

"Notice a triple promise here concerning the security of God's sheep. First, Christ gives them 'eternal' life. Second, they shall 'never' perish, and third, neither shall any pluck them out of Christ's hand." [26]

ANSWER: Jn. 10:28 is a wonderful and true promise, but only as Jesus meant it to be understood! We must examine Jn. 10:27 carefully to understand who "them" and "they" are in verse 28 and what the Lord was saying. It reads, **"My sheep listen to my voice; I know them, and THEY FOLLOW ME."** This is the only type of person, the one that meets these conditions, that will "NEVER PERISH," according to the next verse!

Did you notice the words, "they follow me"? The word translated "follow" is a PRESENT PARTICIPLE in the Greek, which means that it expresses CONTINUOUS OR REPEATED ACTION. In other words, as long as we remain faithful and **CONTINUE** TO FOLLOW JESUS, He will, indeed, assure us that we will "never perish," v.28.

No such promise, however, is given here (or anywhere in the

Bible) to one that would turn and start "to follow Satan" as Paul knew could and did happen (1 Tim. 5:15)! It clearly does NOT cover such. Some read into Jn. 10:28 the words, "under any circumstance" after the words "never perish," but they are NOT there! Jesus did NOT include them in his promise and neither should we!

<u>OBJECTION #2</u>. Can you be "born again" again?

<u>ANSWER:</u> This is a rhetorical question that has confused some. To be "born again" is the same as getting saved or believing in Jesus. Therefore, if one stops believing in Jesus, then later starts believing again, he did indeed get saved again, as Rom. 11:23 declares. Remember also the Prodigal who became "alive again" (Lk. 15:24,32).

<u>OBJECTION #3.</u> Those that truly get saved will faithfully endure to the end and never follow another.

<u>ANSWER:</u> This was **not** true with Demas, Judas, Simon and many others! Furthermore, Jesus clearly taught that one could "believe for a while" then fall away or die (Lk. 8:13)! Paul similarly taught that one could "believe in vain" (1 Cor. 15:2) and fall "away from grace" (Gal. 5:4). Therefore, the wishful position of the U. E. S. proponent here is, again, refuted by the truth of Scripture.

<u>OBJECTION #4.</u> "I tell you the truth, whoever hears my word and believes him who sent me has eternal life and will not be condemned; he has crossed over from death to life," Jn. 5:24. The verse says "will not be condemned." Therefore, one cannot lose it!

<u>ANSWER:</u> Both groups in this controversy agree with this truth that one "will not be condemned" as long as he "has eternal life." However, this isn't even the issue! The issue is, must one remain faithful to the end of his/her life not to be condemned?

The word in Jn. 5:24 rendered "believes" is transliterated as PISTEUON and is also a PRESENT PARTICIPLE in the Greek. Therefore, the Lord is saying here that **we must CONTINUOUSLY BE BELIEVING the Father,** that is, his testimony about Jesus, which implies that Jesus alone is to be the focal point of our TRUST for our soul's salvation. See Matt. 17:5 cf. Jn. 14:6. We will never be condemned, as long as we keep this condition - a continued 100% trusting in Jesus for our soul's salvation.

OBJECTION #5. "The Bible Answer Man" is Hank Hanegraaff. He's on coast to coast radio, he can't be wrong! He wrote the following, "*And remember, eternal life comes to the believer through faith in Christ is not life for two weeks, two months, or even two years; eternal life is everlasting life. It begins at the moment of conversion and stretches on through the eons of time.*"[27]

ANSWER: Hank is right when he writes that eternal life (or salvation) "*comes to the believer through faith in Christ*" and "*begins at the moment of conversion.*" Also, it DOES remain everlasting (or eternal) life. That can't change. However, this doesn't necessitate that we can't be lost after we receive the "gift" of eternal life. In other words, eternal life is the "gift" (Rom. 6:23). As long as we have the gift, we have eternal life. Moreover, as long as we have spiritual life, it is everlasting, but according to Scripture we can still "die" spiritually (Rom. 8:13) and miss the kingdom of God (Gal. 5:19-21)!

OBJECTION #6. We are made sons of God, not put on probation!

ANSWER: Yes, it is true that we become a son of God at the point of salvation (Jn. 1:12). However, "We have come to share in Christ if we hold firmly **TILL THE END** the confidence we had at first," Heb. 3:14. This verse is also true! Better than the word "probation" would be to say: According to Scripture, after salvation, we are sons of God with a free will and the potential of still not inheriting the kingdom of God, because of certain sins, false doctrine about salvation and persecution.

OBJECTION #7. "For God so loved the world that he gave his one and only Son, that whoever believes in him shall not perish but have eternal life," Jn. 3:16. Jesus said "shall not perish"!

ANSWER: The word "believe" is PRESENT PARTICIPLE again! Therefore, Jesus was promising only those that **CONTINUE TO BELIEVE ON HIM** the assurance that they "shall not perish." This verse does NOT cover others that just "believe for a while" then fall away, as Scripture mentions (Lk. 8:13). **Remember, one can truly believe, but this doesn't mean he will always continue to believe on Jesus in the future!**

OBJECTION #8. I agree with Dave Hunt who wrote, *"Salvation is the full pardon by grace from the penalty of all sin, past, present or future...."* [28]

ANSWER: Dave Hunt has done an excellent job exposing and refuting false doctrine and various forms of subtle deceptions that plague the church. However, regarding this subject, we disagree with him.

Yes, we are saved by GRACE. However, the rest of this argument is contrasted by Scripture! See Peter's advice to Simon (Acts 8:22,23); Prov. 28:13 and John's teaching on this subject as cited in 1 Jn. 1:9. This is the Scriptural basis for getting forgiven AFTER initial salvation. **At salvation, all sin to that point is forgiven and forgotten (Lk. 23:42,43; 18:9-14; Acts 10:43-48; Psa. 103:12). However, all sins afterwards committed are NOT automatically covered!** If they were, then Rom. 8:13; Gal. 5:19-21; etc. would be senseless! Furthermore, Jesus clearly taught that our future sins would not be automatically forgiven in **Matt. 6:14,15**!

OBJECTION #9. ***"...love for the one who saved us is the greatest and only acceptable motive for living a holy life...."*** [29]

ANSWER: FEAR, like love, is indeed a legitimate motive or reason for serving God! Jesus told the Twelve when they were about to go out: "Do not be afraid of those who kill the body but cannot kill the soul. Rather, **BE AFRAID** of the one who can destroy both soul and body in Hell," Matt. 10:28. Furthermore, Paul wrote: "...they were broken off because of unbelief, and you stand by faith. Do not be arrogant, but **BE AFRAID**. For if God did not spare the natural branches, he will not spare you either," Rom. 11:20,21. Finally, remember Psa. 2:11, "Serve the Lord with **FEAR** and rejoice with trembling."

OBJECTION #10. God wouldn't save a person then later send him to Hell.

ANSWER: This was not the case for Judas and Saul, the king of Israel! The real truth is God would never force a person to continue to follow Jesus even after his faith in Jesus produced salvation. **Read and ponder Revelation chapters 2 and 3.**

OBJECTION #11. Our fellowship with God can suffer, but never one's relationship as a son.

ANSWER: As "adopted" sons (Eph. 1:5), we can lose our inheritance of the kingdom of God (Gal. 5:21), be disowned by Christ (Matt. 10:33), have our name blotted from the book of life (Rev. 3:5), have our share in the tree of life and New Jerusalem taken away (Rev. 22:19), "DIE" because we chose to live according to the sinful nature (Rom. 8:13) and as the Prodigal **SON,** become "dead" and "lost" (Lk. 15:24)! This obviously describes a much greater loss than just our fellowship with God (or rewards), as some would wishfully like us to believe!

OBJECTION #12. Those that are saved have an inheritance that can "never perish, spoil or fade - kept in heaven" for us (1 Pet. 1:3,4).

ANSWER: This wonderful passage of Scripture only describes our inheritance as Christians. It doesn't say that we cannot annul it through our after-conversion activities and/or beliefs! In fact, just the opposite was repeatedly declared by Paul (Gal. 5:21; 1 Cor. 6:9,10; 15:2; etc.).

OBJECTION #13. Jesus prayed to the Father that He would protect His disciples and that none would be lost. Certainly, the Father heard Jesus' prayer!

ANSWER: The verse referred to is from John 17. This, however, is not a certainty of remaining saved! In the very same prayer, Jesus also prayed for "complete unity" among the believers (Jn. 17:24). Clearly, from 1 Cor. 1:10-13, this didn't occur. Therefore, there must be some unnamed, outside factor to consider here. Remember, it was Jesus Himself who told His disciples that they would have to "stand firm to the end to be saved" on more than one occasion (Matt. 10:22; 24:13) and to "REMAIN" in Him or be thrown into the fire (Jn. 15:4-6)! Also, according to Rom. 8:34, Jesus is now praying for us from the right hand of God. This, however, doesn't mean that His servants cannot be deceived by false teachers, grow lukewarm, fall into impurity, etc. His powerful prayers and **our free will** work together. **Our free will** can, however, override His incredibly powerful prayers and His will for us. This is also evident from the following: It is His will that none should perish (2 Pet. 3:9), yet most will perish (Matt. 7:13,14), in spite of His will!

OBJECTION #14. *"...if salvation from the penalty of breaking God's laws cannot be earned by good deeds, then it CANNOT BE LOST BY BAD DEEDS"* [30] **(emphasis his, but capitalized words are italicized in original).**

ANSWER: This type of statement-conclusion must be carefully examined. Yes, it is true that we don't gain our salvation by good deeds, according to Eph. 2:8,9; Tit. 3:5; 2 Tim. 1:9 and Rom. 4:4-6. However, **the conclusion is FALSE, according to MANY Scriptural passages. See 1 Cor. 6:9,10 and Gal. 5:19-21 just to mention two**. Remember also the many other references cited in this study. (Also, let's call it "sin" not just "bad deeds.")

Please note that sins such as worry and unthankfulness are not listed anywhere in Scripture as being spiritually lethal, as drunkenness, greed, sexual immorality, idolatry, slander and lying are!

OBJECTION #15. A child cannot become unborn, and the relationship of a father and a child cannot be ended. Once a son, always a son.

ANSWER: This argument is based on natural fact, then applied to the spiritual, **which doesn't always hold up as truth**. (U. E. S. adherents frequently make this kind of mistake!) This type of error can be demonstrated by the following facts: Before we became Christians, we were all "children of the devil" (Acts 13:10; 1 Jn. 3:10) and "sons of the evil one" (Matt. 13:38). In other words, the devil was our spiritual father (Jn. 8:44). However, **this spiritual father-child relationship changed** at the point of salvation, according to Scripture! Aren't you glad that spiritual father-child relationships CAN be ended?

Furthermore, many U. E. S. adherents who know the fallacy of the deification of man teaching would be quick to reject one of their arguments which is, likewise, based on natural fact then applied to the spiritual! That faulty argument put forth by Earl Paulk is: "*Dogs have puppies and cats have kittens, so God has little gods.*" [31] Therefore, this type of reasoning must be carefully compared with Scripture.

<u>OBJECTION #16</u>. "...I know whom I have believed, and am convinced that he is able to guard what I have entrusted to him for that day," (2 Tim. 1:12). The only way Paul could have made this statement for himself was if he believed in unconditional eternal security.

<u>ANSWER:</u> Paul certainly knew that a "know-so" salvation existed and that he had it. However, we can assume that Paul believed personally the things he wrote to others. This means that Paul knew his "know-so" salvation at the moment could be negated in the future, as already cited.

Furthermore, Paul obviously believed God would guard or keep him. However, he also knew about the human responsibility for this: "I have fought the good fight, I have finished the race, **<u>I</u> have kept the faith**" (2 Tim. 4:7). Here we see Paul believed in human responsibility too.

<u>OBJECTION #17</u>. A real Christian won't ever be condemned as Romans 8:1 reads, "There is therefore now no condemnation to them which are in Christ Jesus...."

<u>ANSWER:</u> This "no condemnation" mentioned in Rom. 8:1 refers ONLY to those that are in Christ Jesus! This can only be the case if we continue in the faith, for it's definitely possible NOT to remain in the Son (Jn. 15:6; 1 Jn. 2:24; 2 Jn. 9). Furthermore, the K. J. V. renders the "no condemnation" as conditional for only the ones who "walk not after the flesh, but after the Spirit"!

<u>OBJECTION #18.</u> Phil. 1:6 declares, "Being confident of this, that he who began a good work in you will carry it on to completion until the day of Christ Jesus." This proves unconditional eternal security.

<u>ANSWER:</u> The New Testament declares this promise to be true <u>ONLY</u> in the lives of those who meet the conditions stated

elsewhere in Scripture as in Matt. 10:22; Rom. 8:13; Gal. 6:8; etc.

Also, Phil. 1:6 needs to be understood in the light of the context of that book. Phil. 2:12 declares that this church group "always obeyed" in Paul's presence. Though not perfect, this was not a lukewarm, worldly church group, for not only did they "always obey," they were enduring the same types of struggles that Paul had (1:29,30), and they alone helped support Paul financially from the very beginning and were still doing so as this epistle was being written (4:14-16).

Besides the context of the book, the immediate context of the verse CLEARLY shows **WHY** Paul was so "confident," as he states in verse 6, which is really the whole basis of this favorite U. E. S. argument. Verse 7 reads, "It is right for me to feel this way about all of you, **since I have you in my heart....**" Note: **The basis of the "confidence" mentioned in verse 6 was NOT a guaranteed eternal security which all Christians have in common!** The basis of Paul's "confidence" mentioned in verse 6 was that he had them "IN HIS HEART" - meaning they would be aided in their personal struggles by his heart felt prayers cited in verses 9-11. Note the same phrase mentioned in verse 6, "until the day of Christ Jesus" is repeated in verse 10 as "until the day of Christ," which connects Paul's "confidence" for them to his prayers for them.

<u>OBJECTION #19.</u> Samson was sexually immoral and he's mentioned as a hero in Hebrews 11. Therefore, one can be sexually immoral, like him, and be saved.

<u>ANSWER:</u> It's true that Samson is mentioned in Heb. 11:32, and why he was included in this chapter is mentioned in verse 34. This, however, has nothing to do with the conclusion that one can be sexually immoral and be saved. **The Apostle Paul, in no uncertain terms, stated that the sexually immoral are wicked, impure, and God rejecters who will <u>NOT</u> inherit the kingdom of God (1 Cor. 6:9,10; Gal. 5:19-21; Eph. 5:5,6; 1 Thess. 4:3-8). Furthermore, God Himself declared that the sexually immoral will go to the fiery lake of burning sulfur (Rev. 21:5-<u>8</u>). Samson, David and/or any living person today is no exception!**

<u>OBJECTION #20.</u> Fritz Ridenour has done an excellent job showing the differences between Roman Catholicism and true Christianity in his book, in which he also cites 1 Pet. 1:5 for support of U. E. S.[32] I believe both points.

<u>ANSWER:</u> Ridenour is absolutely correct about those differences between Catholicism and true Christianity, including their false plan of salvation, which has misled hundreds of millions of sincere Catholics into a dangerous, spiritual deception. For this he needs to be commended, especially in this day of rampant, ecumenical compromise with Catholicism for the sake of personal ministry. However, it's unfortunate that he would taint his excellent book by trying to support U. E. S.!

1 Pet. 1:5 says, "Who **through faith**, are shielded by God's power until the coming of the salvation that is ready to be revealed in the last time." The key words in this verse are, "through faith." This verse shows the shield of protection that believers have exists ONLY as long as we keep the faith! The Lord taught this is certainly no guarantee, though, with His words, "They believe for a while, but in time of testing they fall away," Lk. 8:13. Also, Paul wrote, "But they were broken off because of unbelief, and you stand by faith. Do not be arrogant, but be afraid. For if God did not spare the natural branches, he will not spare you either....sternness to those who fell, but kindness to you, provided that you continue in his kindness. Otherwise, you also will be cut off," Rom. 11:20-22.

<u>OBJECTION #21.</u> 1 Jn. 3:9 says, "No one who is born of God will continue to sin, because God's seed remains in him; he cannot go on sinning, because he has been born of God." This seems clear to me that someone truly saved can't go back to a life of sin.

<u>ANSWER:</u> In part, this verse deals with initial salvation, which frees one from sin's slavery and changes his desire for sin. However, to conclude from this verse that one can't go back to a

life of sin is error as the Biblical examples of Solomon, the younger widows of 1 Tim. 5:11-15, those referred to in 2 Pet. 2:20-22, etc. show! "God's seed," His Word, impedes sin IF HIDDEN IN OUR HEART (Psa. 119:9-11). However, as one might not "remain" in the Vine (Jn. 15:6), God's seed might not "remain" in the person who gets born of God! If 1 Jn. 3:9 had the meaning the U. E. S. advocates give it, then Paul's multiple warnings to the Christians would be meaningless (Gal. 5:19-21)!

OBJECTION #22. I believe in U. E. S. because I believe in the finished work of Christ!

ANSWER: The writer of Hebrews certainly believed in the finished work of Christ also (Heb. 7:27; 9:26; 10:11-14)! This, however, didn't mean he believed in U. E. S. as well (Heb. 3:12-14; 6:4-6; 10:26-31)! The same can be said elsewhere (Rom. 6:10 cf. Rom. 8:13; Gal. 5:19-21; 2 Tim. 2:12; etc.).

Such U. E. S. proponents infer that it is impossible to believe in the finished work of Christ and not believe in U. E. S. at the same time, in an effort to immediately discredit the opposing view. Obviously, they are wrong, according to what was just cited. The finished work of Christ is foundational to Christianity, but irrelevant in this controversy regarding the believer's security.

OBJECTION #23. I know I am eternally secure because God has promised that He will never leave me and never forsake me.

ANSWER: This is quoted from Heb. 13:5b which is taken from the Old Testament reference of Deut. 31:6,8. Though God's promise to Israel in Deut. 31 verses 6 and 8 is that He [God] will never "forsake" them, about ten verses later in the same chapter God predicts Israel will "forsake" Him, then in verse 17 He said, "On that day I will become angry with them and **forsake** them; I will hide my face from them, and they will be destroyed. Many

DISASTERS AND DIFFICULTIES will come upon them, and on that day they will ask, 'Have not these disasters come upon us because our God is not with us?' And I will certainly hide my face on that day because of all their wickedness in turning to other gods." **[This is a conditional promise, as the whole chapter bears out, which can be nullified by "wickedness." If we "forsake" God by turning to wickedness, He will "forsake" us!]**

What does it mean then to be **forsaken** by God here? When this occurred, various "calamities" came upon them: wasting famine, consuming pestilence, deadly plague, wild beasts, vipers and sword, according to Deut. 32:23-25. Therefore, the U. E. S. people read into this Scripture found in Heb. 13 something that is not there, for it does not even deal with an assured and guaranteed entrance into the kingdom of God at all, but instead a promise for temporal protection and well-being only, which can be negated by sin!

OBJECTION #24. Samson committed suicide and he went to heaven because he is listed in the faith chapter. Therefore, we know Christians can likewise commit this awful sin and still go to heaven.

ANSWER: Samson did not commit suicide. His prayer shows he asked God to let him die with the Philistines, but left the matter entirely in God's hands (Jdg. 16:28-30). **Unlike Samson, suicide victims take into their own hands the termination of their own physical lives.** God honored Samson's prayer, but didn't honor Jonah's prayer for the same (Jonah 4:3) nor Elijah's prayer (1 Ki. 19:4)!

OBJECTION #25. If I'm wrong as a U. E. S. advocate, I want to be wrong because I overemphasize the infinite work of Christ on the cross.

ANSWER: This sounds like a good reason to accept U. E. S. or stay with this position. However, the infinite work of Christ, as just shown, doesn't relate to this controversy! Advocates of both positions believe in the infinite work of Christ. Truth is the deciding factor, which shows U. E. S. is a myth that holds its adherents in a false security with obvious spiritual disadvantages.

8

??? ? ?

Bible Quiz

* Questions for Teachable U. E. S. Proponents *

1. Are the Holy Scriptures or the majority of popular teachers who hold to a particular doctrine the deciding factor that makes that doctrine correct (2 Tim. 3:16,17)? ____The Holy Scriptures ____Majority of popular teachers.

(See Lk. 15:11-32 for #2 - #10)

2. Was the Prodigal Son "dead" and "lost" when he was sexually immoral? ____YES ____NO.

3. Could that death be physical? ____YES ____NO.

4. Did anyone or anything "pluck" him out of the Father's hand as promised in Jn. 10:28? ____YES ____NO.

5. Did the Father let him, of his own free will, walk out on him which led to his "dead" and "lost" condition? ____YES ____NO.

6. Is the promise of not being snatched out of Jesus' hand (Jn. 10:28) in reference ONLY to those who are **FOLLOWING** Jesus, verse 27? ____YES ____NO.

7. Though the Prodigal Son was "sealed" as a son, did that mean he was always saved, even when he was in sexual immorality? (See also 1 Cor. 6:9,10; Rev. 21:8; 22:15.) ____YES ____NO.

8. Does the Bible say we are "sealed" unto the day of redemption or "saved" unto the day of redemption (Eph. 4:30)? ____"Sealed" unto the day ____"Saved" unto the day.

9. Can they be the same in the light of the Prodigal Son, Demas, Judas and others? ____YES ____NO.

10. In regards to Heb. 13:5, did the Father "leave" or "forsake" the Prodigal or did the Prodigal "leave" and "forsake" the Father? ____Father left ____Prodigal left.

11. If we reject God will He likewise reject us (Deut. 32:15 cf. v.19)? ___YES ___NO.

12. We show we reject God by not living holy lives (1 Thess. 4:7,8). ___TRUE ___FALSE.

13. "...The LORD is with you when you are with him. If you seek him, he will be found by you, but **if you forsake him, he will forsake you," 2 Chron. 15:2**. What condition must we meet for God to "forsake" us? ______________________.

14. Are the phrases "once saved always saved" or "once in grace always in grace" actually quoted **anywhere** in the entire Bible? ___YES ___NO.

15. According to 1 Cor. 6:9,10 and Rev. 21:8, are all drunkards, all the sexually immoral, all greedy and all liars **UNSAVED**, regardless who they are with no exceptions? ___YES ___NO.

16. Are all homosexuals **UNSAVED**, according to **1 Cor. 6:9,10**; Rom. 1:27; Gen. 19:4,5 cf. Jude 7 and Lev. 20:13? ___YES ___NO.

(See Lk. 8:5-15 and Matt. 13:3-23
for #17 - #23)

17. According to Jesus, do some people "believe for a while" then cease believing? ___YES ___NO.

18. Is the "falling away," which these same people experience in this parable, equated to the plant dying? ___ YES ___NO.

19. Did their initial belief (or faith) produce life? ___YES ___NO.

20. Was this life **spiritual** since it was produced by the Word of God and came as a result of their own personal faith? ___YES ___NO.

21. Was it persecution over the Word of God which caused this type of person to "fall away" or die? ___YES ___NO.

22. Is persecution a "test" that will cause some true Christians to "fall away" or die spiritually? ___YES ___NO.

23. Are the notes in a study Bible inspired, like the actual Scriptures, or can these notes reflect the erroneous views of the commentator/s? ___The notes are inspired ___The notes can be wrong.

(See 2 Pet. 2:20-22 for #24 - #29)

24. Did the people Peter wrote of "escape the corruption of the

world by knowing our Lord and Savior Jesus Christ?" ___YES ___NO.

25. Did they know "the way of righteousness" before they were entangled in sin for the second time? ___YES ___NO.

26. According to Matt. 21:32 is Jesus "the way of righteousness" as implied by Matt. 3:11 cf. Jn. 1:29-34? ___ YES ___NO.

27. Were these people at one time "washed" when they knew the way of righteousness and escaped the corruption of the world by knowing Jesus Christ? ___YES ___NO.

28. At salvation are we "washed" in Jesus' blood (1 Cor. 6:11; Rev. 7:14)? ___YES ___NO.

29. Could the people Peter wrote of have been "washed" in anything other than Jesus' blood? ___YES ___NO.

30. Is it possible to "lose" (K. J. V.) or "forfeit" (N. I. V.) your soul, according to Jesus (Mk. 8:36)? ___YES ___NO.

31. Are disciples of Christ likened unto salt that can "lose" its saltiness to the point that it is "no longer good for anything" (Lk. 14:34)? ___YES ___NO.

32. According to the Bible, what makes us strong (Acts 20:32)? ___Persecution ___Word of God.

33. Did Jesus say "many" will turn away from the Christian faith at the end of the age because of persecution (Matt. 24:9,10)? ___YES ___NO.

34. Does the STANDING FIRM "TO THE END," as mentioned in Matt. 10:22, refer to remaining faithful to Jesus during persecution, without disowning him? ___YES ___NO.

35. Is it possible for a real Christian to "believe in vain" (1 Cor. 15:1,2)? ___YES ___NO.

36. How can a Christian "believe in vain" (1 Cor. 15:1,2)? ____.

37. Did Jesus teach twice, "He who stands firm to the end will be saved" <u>or</u> "He who stands firm to the end will not lose his rewards" (Matt. 10:22; 24:13)? ___Will be saved ___Will not lose his rewards.

38. Did Paul **REPEATEDLY WARN <u>TRUE</u> CHRISTIANS** that certain sinful activities would cause them to "not inherit the kingdom of God" (Gal. 5:19-<u>21</u>)? ___YES ___NO.

39. Is sin, therefore, still an "issue"? ___YES ___NO.

40. When Paul taught this did he know that "neither death nor life, neither angels nor demons, neither the present nor the future,

nor any powers, neither height nor depth nor anything else in all creation" could separate the Galatian Christians from the love of God that is in Christ Jesus as stated in Rom. 8:38,39? ___YES, HE WROTE THOSE VERSES ___NO.

41. Is it, therefore, possible that he understood Rom. 8:38,39 to mean a Christian is unconditionally and eternally secure in the light of Gal. 5:19-21? ___YES ___NO.

42. Was Paul a "grace" teacher in the truest sense? ___YES ___NO.

43. Did Paul fight against legalism (Gal. 5:2-4)? ___YES ___NO.

44. Could such a warning as issued in Gal. 5:21 be legalistic if, similarly, spoken directly to real Christians today? ___YES ___NO.

45. Was Paul contradicting his "freedom" in Christ message by teaching Gal. 5:19-21? ___YES ___NO.

46. Paul wrote, "You, my brothers, were called to be free. But **do not use your freedom to indulge the sinful nature**; rather serve one another in love," Gal. 5:13. Under Paul's freedom or liberty message as concisely cited here, did he allow for an occasional getting drunk or act of sexual immorality? ___YES ___NO.

47. Peter wrote, "Live as free men, but **do not use your freedom as a cover-up for evil**; live as servants of God," 1 Pet. 2:16. Under the Apostle Peter's freedom message, did he allow for an occasional getting drunk or act of sexual immorality, as some say is "permissible"? ___YES ___NO.

48. Does it follow then, if someone teaches a "freedom" or liberty message that they say allows for an occasional getting drunk or act of sexual immorality, that he is a false teacher which should be openly refuted? ___YES ___NO.

49. Does the true Biblical grace or liberty message mean: you believe on Christ, then go do whatever you want? ___YES ___NO.

50. Are God's commands "burdensome" (1 Jn. 5:3)? ___YES ___NO.

51. Was it advantageous for Christians to hear Paul's repeated warning of the possibility of them still "not inheriting the kingdom of God," as cited in Gal. 5:19-21? ___YES ___NO.

52. On the other hand, do you suppose Christians today are at a disadvantage when they don't get directed at them the type of warning cited in Gal. 5:19-21? ___YES ___NO.

53. Should ALL true "grace" teachers be issuing this same type

of warning today? ___YES ___NO.

54. Have you ever heard a U. E. S. teacher issue to Christians the same type of warning as Gal. 5:21 which Paul repeatedly gave? ___YES ___NO.

55. Is it an **impossibility** for them to do so? ___YES ___NO.

56. The Apostle Paul wrote, "This righteousness from God comes through faith in Jesus Christ to all who **believe**," Rom. 3:22. The Greek reveals that the word "believe" used here is a continuous tense. If one does not continue in this belief, would he then meet this God-given condition for salvation? ___YES ___NO.

57. Did Paul believe that a true Christian could "fall away from grace" (Gal. 5:4)? ___YES ___NO.

58. Is it logical for the U. E. S. proponent to accuse the other side of teaching a works salvation, since Paul, the grace teacher, obviously taught in opposition to their view (Rom. 8:13; 1 Cor. 15:2; Gal. 5:2-4; 6:8,9; etc.)? ___YES ___NO.

59. Did Paul believe that a true Christian could be deceived doctrinally to the point where "Christ will be of **NO VALUE**" to him at all (Gal. 5:2)? ___YES ___NO.

60. Did the Apostle John teach that believing certain false doctrine could cause the Christian **NOT** to remain in Christ (1 Jn. 2:24; 2 Jn. 9)? ___YES ___NO.

61. Is it possible for a Christian to "become an enemy of God" **again** (Jam. 4:4)? ___YES ___NO.

62. Will raging fire consume the "enemies of God" (Heb. 10:27)? ___YES ___NO.

63. Who were Hymenaeus and Philetus (2 Tim. 2:17,18)? ____.

64. Did Paul personally know of some younger Christian widows who turned from Jesus and started to "**follow Satan**" (1 Tim. 5:11-15)? ___YES ___ NO.

65. Do you think if some present-day U. E. S. proponents would have observed these same younger Christian widows that Paul referred to they would have possibly concluded that those women were never really saved to begin with? ___YES ___NO.

66. Did Paul personally know of some Christians who were "eager for money" and consequently wandered from the Christian faith (1 Tim. 6:10)? ___YES ___NO.

67. Did Jesus teach that **FRUITLESS CHRISTIANS ARE IN DANGER OF BEING "THROWN INTO THE FIRE AND BURNED" (JN. 15:1-6)?** ___YES ___NO.

68. Did Jesus teach that **LUKEWARM CHRISTIANS ARE IN DANGER OF BEING EXPELLED FROM THE BODY OF CHRIST (REV. 3:15,16)?** ___YES ___NO.

69. Did Jesus teach that we must be **FAITHFUL "TO THE POINT OF DEATH"** to receive the crown of life (Rev. 2:10)? ___YES ___NO.

70. **ALL who inherit the kingdom of God receive the crown of life.** We know this since the crown of life is promised to those who truly love God (Jam. 1:12) and those who truly love God will inherit the kingdom of God (Jam. 2:5). It is not something that only some Christians will merit, as taught by the U. E. S. teachers. ___ TRUE ___FALSE.

71. Did the Lord Jesus teach that **UNFORGIVENESS IN THE HEART OF A CHRISTIAN CAN NEGATE HIS OWN FORGIVENESS FROM GOD (MATT. 6:14,15; 18:21-35)?** ___YES ___NO.

72. Should we discount this teaching on the basis that it was given before the cross? ___YES ___NO.

73. Did Jesus teach, "You must be born again" before the cross (Jn. 3:7)? ___YES ___NO.

74. Did Jesus teach if we are ashamed of him, he'll likewise be ashamed of us (Lk. 9:26)? ___YES ___NO.

75. Did Jesus teach if we disown him before men, he'll likewise **disown** us before the Father (Matt. 10:33)? ___YES ___NO.

76. **How can one still be saved, if Jesus "disowns" him/her?** ____.

77. Would it be possible for Jesus to "disown" us if we were never owned by him first? ___YES ___NO.

78. Did Paul also teach the same truth as Jesus did in Matt. 10:33 to others (2 Tim. 2:12)? ___YES ___NO.

79. Could Paul have been teaching "legalism" or "bondage" in doing so? ___YES ___NO.

80. Did Paul want Christians to "**be afraid**" regarding their spiritual position (Rom. 11:20,21)? ___YES ___NO.

81. Could he have been trying to create an unwarranted fear in them? ___YES ___NO.

82. In light of Rom. 11:20,21, did Paul dangerously overemphasize the "assurance" doctrine as some are today? ___YES ___NO.

83. Does SIN "separate" us from God (Isa. 59:2)? ___YES ___NO.

84. Can sin separate the true Christian from God to the point

where he DIES spiritually and misses the kingdom of God (Rom. 8:13; Lk. 15:24,32; Gal. 6:8)? ___YES ___NO.

85. Paul declared that if a Christian lives according to the sinful nature he will definitely "**DIE**" (Rom. 8:13). Can this death be physical death, which would imply that if we would not live according to the sinful nature we would not "die" physically? ___YES, it's physical death ___NO, it can't be physical death.

86. Must the "**DIE**" in Rom. 8:13 be spiritual death? ___YES ___NO.

87. Is it possible to "die" spiritually if you were never first alive spiritually? ___YES ___NO.

88. Does the Bible teach a **HUMAN RESPONSIBILITY** for the Christian race (Col. 3:5; 1 Tim. 5:22; 1 Pet. 2:1; 1 Jn. 5:21; etc.)? ___YES ___NO.

89. Did Jesus say we must obey his commands to remain in his love (Jn. 15:10)? ___YES ___NO.

90. **The "unbelieving" are NOT the only ones that will end up in the lake of fire (Rev. 21:8).** ___TRUE ___FALSE.

91. The Bible ends with a warning to Christians, that is, their share in the tree of life and New Jerusalem can potentially be removed (Rev. 22:18,19). ___TRUE ___FALSE.

92. If a Christian during the reign of the Antichrist yields to the heavy pressure and receives the mark of the beast and worships his image, what will be his/her eternal future state (Rev. 14:9-12)? ____.

93. Does this passage contradict U. E. S.? ___YES ___NO.

94. If a Christian sows to please his sinful nature, will he reap DESTRUCTION as opposed to eternal life (Gal. 6:8)? ___YES ___NO.

95. Must a real, Bible-defined Christian "**hold firmly TILL THE END**" the confidence he had at first to share in Christ (Heb. 3:14)? ___YES ___NO.

96. Did Paul, the grace teacher, say: "Don't you know that when you offer yourselves to someone to obey him as slaves, you are slaves to the one whom you obey - whether you are slaves to sin, which leads to **DEATH**, or to obedience, which leads to righteousness?" (Rom. 6:16). ___YES ___NO.

97. **Does true grace teaching promote holy living** (Tit. 2:12)? ___ YES ___NO.

98. On the other hand, can false grace teaching promote immorality (Jude 4)? ___YES ___NO.

99. **In your opinion, is holy living or immorality promoted by**

the teaching that went out across the United States, that is, fornication is "permissible" but not "profitable"? ____HOLY LIVING ____IMMORALITY.

100. **In your opinion, is holy living or immorality promoted by the teaching that David's sins of adultery and murder did NOT negate his salvation? ____HOLY LIVING ____IMMORALITY.**

101. Is this view of David's sins not negating his salvation a part of the unconditional eternal security doctrine? ____YES ____NO.

102. Are the more moderate U. E. S. proponents unwittingly stating that David was NEVER REALLY SAVED, since he committed sins of adultery and murder? ____YES ____NO.

103. Are Jesus' "disciples" saved (Lk. 14:26-33)? ____YES ____NO.

104. Was Judas once a "disciple" of Christ (Matt. 10:1)? ____YES ____NO.

105. Therefore, was Judas once saved? ____ YES ____NO.

106. Did Judas go to Hell after he committed suicide (Mk. 14:21)? ____YES ____NO.

107. Is suicide really self-murder that cannot be repented of? ____YES ____NO.

108. Will ALL murderers go to the lake of fire (Rev. 21:8)? ____YES ____NO.

109. In the natural, we as heirs receive our inheritance when the giver dies. This, however, is not so in the spiritual! To receive our inheritance of the kingdom we must "overcome" (Rev. 21:7). _____ TRUE _____FALSE.

110. Can unconditional eternal security be true in either of its two forms? ____YES ____NO.

111. Is unconditional eternal security a "*glorious truth*" or a myth that needs to be boldly addressed and openly refuted as never before? ____Glorious truth ____MYTH that needs to be boldly addressed and openly refuted as never before.

112. According to the Bible, is it teachers proclaiming truth or teachers proclaiming falsehood that are "divisive" (Rom. 16:17)? ____Teachers proclaiming truth ____Teachers proclaiming falsehood.

113. Can you understand why many Christians, who firmly believe we are saved at the moment of a trusting and submitting faith in Jesus Christ, do not believe in unconditional eternal security and openly speak out against it for the sake of truth? ____YES ____NO.

9

* Truths About Salvation *

A We are saved by **GRACE** and **MERCY**, and NOT by our own good deeds, water baptism, the sacraments, church membership, Saturday Sabbath-keeping, Mary, the Ten Commandments, the Golden Rule, lodge membership, etc. (Acts 4:12; 15:11; Rom. 4:4-6; Eph. 2:8,9; 2 Tim. 1:9; Tit. 3:5). However, a saving faith in Jesus will **ALWAYS** have corresponding good deeds (Jn. 5:29; Jam. 2:14; 1 Jn. 2:3,4). Rom. 2:7 says, "To those **who by PERSISTENCE IN DOING GOOD** seek glory, honor and immortality, he will give eternal life."

B Salvation or eternal life comes **instantly** (Lk. 23:42,43; Acts 10:43-48; 1 Jn. 5:12) at the point of turning to God in **REPENTANCE** and having **FAITH** in Jesus Christ (Acts 20:21). To be a member of the Lord's church you must **SUBMIT** TO CHRIST (Eph. 5:24a). Similarly, Gal. 5:24 reads, "Those who belong to Christ Jesus **have crucified** the sinful nature with its passions and desires."

Remember this: the word "believe" as used in Rom. 3:22 and many other places is a <u>CONTINUOUS TENSE IN THE GREEK</u>! This verse reads: "This righteousness from God comes through faith in Jesus Christ to all who **believe.**" Since this is a continuous tense, if you start off believing, but don't end up believing, **THEN YOU DIDN'T MEET THE BIBLICAL CONDITION FOR SALVATION** which, according to Lk. 8:13 and 1 Cor. 15:2, is clearly a possibility! Similarly, this same **CONTINUOUS TENSE** for "believe" is also shown in the often-quoted Jn. 6:47 verse: "I tell you the truth, he who **believes** has everlasting life." Finally, in Jn. 6:29, Jesus answered the question presented in the preceding verse: "What must we do to do the works God requires?" The Wuest translation, cited for its clarity here, renders this, "Answered Jesus and said to them, This is the work of God, that you **continually be**

believing on Him whom that One sent off on a mission."

Remember also this link between repentance and faith: One can't get forgiven unless he believes on the name of Jesus (Acts 10:43); yet **one can't get forgiven unless he REPENTS (Acts 3:19).** Moreover, unless one believes on Jesus he will perish (Jn. 3:16); yet, **unless one REPENTS he will perish (Lk. 13:3,5). REPENTANCE, therefore, is inseparable with FAITH in Jesus that saves from the lake of fire.**

The word "repent" means to "**turn from your evil ways,**" according to the Lord Jesus, and **NOT** merely just A CHANGE OF MIND as some teach! We know this because Jesus said the Ninevites REPENTED at the preaching of Jonah (Matt. 12:41), which is equated to the Ninevites **TURNING FROM THEIR EVIL WAYS** (Jonah 3:10). This is what Jesus said we **MUST** do or we would perish (Lk. 13:3)! Also, sorrow for our sins precedes true repentance, 2 Cor. 7:10.

True believers in Christ are <u>COMMITTED</u> to the Lord. This is shown by a combination of both Scripture and logic. If A = B, and B = C, then A = C. In other words, if a "believer" and "disciple" of Christ are the same (premise A), and disciples are committed to Jesus (premise B), then true believers are committed to Jesus (conclusion). Premise A (a believer in Christ is a disciple of Christ) is proven by the following: The words "believer" and "disciple" (in reference to Jesus' disciples) are used interchangeably (Acts 9:1 cf. Acts 22:19). Also, one must be a "disciple" to qualify for Christian baptism (Matt. 28:19). Yet, elsewhere in Scripture we see that one is qualified for Christian baptism at the point of believing in Jesus (Acts 8:12,13; 16:31-33). Premise B (disciples of Christ are committed people) is proven by Lk. 14:26,27,<u>33</u>. The logical conclusion is: **true believers in Christ are <u>COMMITTED</u> people who have repented and are TRUSTING IN, CLINGING TO, AND RELYING UPON Jesus Christ <u>100%</u> for their soul's salvation. They have much more than just an intellectual assent to the historical facts surrounding Jesus Christ - His death, burial and resurrection.**

C Our hearts, if purified, were purified **BY FAITH IN JESUS CHRIST** (Rom. 3:22; Acts 15:9). We are also sanctified **BY FAITH IN JESUS CHRIST** and the **Word of God** (Acts 26:18; Jn. 17:17). Therefore, sanctification is also progressive.

D At the point of salvation, we are cleansed from all our past sins (2 Pet. 1:9). Simultaneously and instantly, our sins were also **FORGIVEN** and **FORGOTTEN** from God's perspective (Heb. 8:12). Our past sins have been separated from us as far as the east is from the west (Psa. 103:12) and hurled into the depths of the sea (Mic. 7:19), as far as God is concerned.

After salvation, certain sins of commission and/or omission are **automatically** cleansed by Jesus' blood (1 Jn. 1:7), if we meet the cited condition of walking in the light as He is in the light.

Other sins, committed after salvation, **need to be confessed directly to God to be forgiven** (1 Jn. 1:9). An **attitude of repentance is understood** based on Prov. 28:13. In other words, your future sins are not all automatically forgiven at the point of initial salvation, as some are saying.

Finally, **every time a Christian sins, he does NOT have to get saved again.** Jesus said, "A person who has had a bath needs only to wash his feet" (Jn. 13:10). This is done by applying 1 Jn. 1:9.

E "He who has the Son has life; he who does not have the Son of God does not have life," 1 Jn. 5:12. **Please notice the CONTINUOUS tense that is shown in the word "has."** That verse does NOT say, "He who **HAD** the Son has life." We have life only as long as we have Jesus (Jn. 14:6).

F Paul and John knew they were saved before they died, as they also knew others were saved (2 Tim. 1:9; 1 Jn. 3:1; etc.). We can have this assurance too.

G Once we are saved, we do **NOT** stay saved by our own good deeds! Gal. 3:3 is very important here: "Are you so foolish? After beginning with the Spirit, are you now trying to attain your goal by human effort?" **In question form, Paul denounces the idea of staying saved by good deeds.** If we try to remain saved this way after salvation then Paul's statement in Gal. 5:4 will apply to us: "You who are trying to be justified by law have been alienated from Christ; you have fallen away from grace." **The KEY is to continue to sincerely TRUST Jesus 100% for your salvation to the place where you are living holy and NOT committing the soul-damning sins listed in Scripture (such as 1 Cor. 6:9,10; Gal. 5:19-21; Eph. 5:5; Rev. 21:8 and 22:15), that is, the ones that will send ANYONE to Hell, even a person who was once saved.**

H We stay saved by continuing to "follow" Jesus (Jn. 10:27). To put this in Paul's words: "...A man reaps what he sows. The one who sows to please his sinful nature, from that nature will reap destruction; **the one who sows to please the Spirit, from the Spirit <u>will reap eternal life</u>," Gal. 6:7,8.**

To remain faithful to Jesus, we also must not love our own physical lives to the point where we shrink from death! This martyr's attitude is not just for some, but for all Christians! Rev. 12:11 says, "They overcame him by the blood of the Lamb and by the word of their testimony; **they did not love their lives so much as to shrink from death.**" Remember also Matt. 10:28.

There is the power of God, **coupled with human responsibility**, that will enable us to remain faithful! Rom. 8:13 is clear on this: "For if you live according to the sinful nature, you will die; but if by the Spirit **YOU** put to death the misdeeds of the body, you will live."

I We **MUST** "stand firm to **THE END** to be saved" (Matt. 10:22; 24:13). In other words, we started our Christian race, that is, a long-distance marathon race, at the point of salvation. Now we must finish our race to reach our "goal," which is the salvation of our souls (1 Pet. 1:9). Please note Paul's words carefully: "But now he has reconciled you by Christ's physical body through death to present you holy in his sight, without blemish and free from accusation - **<u>IF</u> you continue in your faith**, established and firm, not moved from the hope held out in the gospel.

THIS IS THE GOSPEL THAT YOU HEARD and that has been proclaimed to every creature under heaven, and of which I, Paul, have become a servant," Col. 1:22,23. **NOTE: Paul's gospel implies that we might NOT CONTINUE IN OUR FAITH! Remember 1 Cor. 15:1,2.**

J There are three tenses in salvation: **PAST** (Eph. 2:8,9), **PRESENT** (1 Cor. 1:18; 2 Cor. 2:15) and **FUTURE** (Mk. 10:30; Gal. 6:8 and Phil. 1:28). This is like saying you HAD a driver's license last year, you HAVE it now and SHALL HAVE it in the future, if you don't forfeit it by getting caught breaking certain driving laws, etc. You must CONTINUE to obey these traffic laws to not have your driver's license revoked! Similarly, there are conditions for Christians, since we are NOT yet actually in Paradise with the Lord! You might be on the road to Heaven with eternal life now, but you can still miss it and end up in Hell, as **many** have in the past (Jn. 6:66) and will in the future (Matt. 25:1-13).

K **WALK IN FEAR.** Paul wrote: "...You do not support the root, but the root supports you. You will say then, 'Branches were broken off so that I could be grafted in.' Granted. But they were broken off **because of UNBELIEF, and you stand BY FAITH. Do NOT be arrogant, but BE AFRAID. For if God did not spare the natural branches, he will not spare you either.** Consider therefore the KINDNESS and STERNNESS of God: sternness to those who fell, but kindness to you, **provided that you CONTINUE in his kindness. Otherwise, you also WILL BE CUT OFF.** And if they do not persist in UNBELIEF, they will be grafted in, for God is able to graft them in **AGAIN**," Rom. 11:18-23.

Yes, there is an assurance for the Christian, but only for the one who **CONTINUES** in faith. This section of Holy Writ from Romans was cited to promote the real truth about assurance, which should cause one to walk in a holy **FEAR** of God!

In contrast to Paul's "assurance" message, many today are teaching things which tend to remove all fear of God and sin and promote the "arrogance" which is condemned by this God-given passage!

L A weak Christian needs to be strengthened spiritually. This should be his **top priority**, since he/she is NOT unconditionally, eternally secure! Meditating in and memorizing the Scriptures, **with a sincere desire to change accordingly**, is the best way to do this. Also, stay in an attitude of prayer throughout the day and fellowship with other true Christians, as often as your schedule permits. It is possible to be spiritually "wretched, pitiful, poor, blind and naked" and still be saved for a time, as Rev. 3:17 shows. However, this spiritual condition is very serious! Jesus said such need to "be earnest and repent" (v.19)! Be sure to read over chapter 12.

M "Now these things occurred as examples, **to keep us from setting our hearts on evil things** as they did. Do not be idolaters, as some of them were; as it is written: 'The people sat down to eat and drink and got up to indulge in pagan revelry.'

We should not commit sexual immorality, as some of them did and in one day twenty-three thousand of them died. We should not test the Lord, as some of them did - and were killed by snakes. And do not grumble, as some of them did - and were killed by the destroying angel. These things happened to them as examples and were written down as **warnings for us**, on whom the fulfillment of the ages has come. So, **if you think you are STANDING FIRM, BE CAREFUL THAT YOU DON'T FALL,**" 1 Cor. 10:6-12!

Again, in contrast to U. E. S., Paul **WARNED** about a dangerous mentality, that is, a type of over-confidence of "standing firm" that sets one up for a "fall." None are more convinced than the U. E. S. adherents about their secure or firm position in Christ. **Beyond this obvious deception lies a danger to "fall" because of such, according to 1 Cor. 10:12!**

10

⁎ How Much Will God Put Up With? ⁎

Shockingly, **there is a type of Christian that sickens Jesus!** This kind of Christian existed in first century Christianity and still exists today. The Lord spoke of him in Rev. 3:14-22. Such a child of God is "neither cold nor hot" for the things of God - prayer meetings, Bible studies, Christian fellowship, tithing, communion, soul winning, helping the widows, orphans, poor, aged, sick, weak, etc. They don't really "**crave**" God's word, which is needed for spiritual growth (1 Pet. 2:2)! They aren't "**devoted**" to the apostle's teaching and to the fellowship, to the breaking of bread and to prayer (Acts 2:42). They obey in thought, word and deed **only when it's convenient.** When it's not so convenient to obey, **they don't. In other words, THEY ARE COMMITTED ONLY TO THE POINT OF THEIR OWN CONVENIENCE,** which constantly varies. Their spiritual temperature is "lukewarm," that is, sometimes hot and sometimes cold, but **never faithfully** one or the other. (To understand "lukewarmness" better, consider what an equal amount of hot and cold water mixed together would yield.)

The amazing thing about the "lukewarm" is that they don't recognize their need or the DANGER they are in! In their "wretched, pitiful, poor, blind and naked" spiritual condition, THEY THINK they "do not need a thing," they are this deceived! Therefore, the NEED TO CHANGE is hidden from their "blinded" eyes and ISN'T THE PRIORITY IT SHOULD BE! Imagine being in such DANGER and thinking all is well! This, in fact, is reality for MANY in our modern day!

Surprisingly, **whole congregations can be in this condition,** as was the case at Laodicea in John's day. Perhaps the environment of the city of Laodicea helped lull the Christians there into this disgusting, spiritual condition. It was a banking center that was also known for its manufacture of rich garments of black wool and its medical school that made powder for the treatment of eye troubles. (This may explain the counsel Jesus gave about "riches," "garments" and "eye salve.") **Ease, comfort** and **pleasure** were things those Christians were accustomed to then, like Christians in America are today!

What kind of DANGER were they in? They were on the verge of being "spit" out of Jesus' mouth, verse 16! The Greek word is actually **"vomit."** Soon these lukewarm Christians would be **expelled from the Body of Christ** in much the same way that something would be that nauseates our stomach and must be expelled to bring relief. This was their promised future, **if they would choose to ignore Jesus' counsel to "be earnest and repent."** The patient and slow-to-anger Lord couldn't stand any more and issued His ultimatum in the form of a warning. Then, **as now,** the half-hearted, apathetic, satisfied and "lukewarm" were forced to make their **MOST IMPORTANT** decision, **a decision that would affect the continuation OR THE TERMINATION of their spiritual life.**

Jesus said, "I know your deeds, that you are neither cold nor hot. **I wish you were either one or the other!** So, because you are lukewarm - neither hot nor cold - I am about to spit you out of my mouth," Rev. 3:15,16. According to this, Jesus' preference scale goes from **HOT** at the top, to **COLD** in the middle, to **LUKEWARM** at the bottom. The word translated **"HOT"** in the Greek means: **boiled, boiling, glowing with zeal and fervent.** In other words, Jesus wanted them (as He wants us) to be **BOILING HOT all the time!** This isn't a great revelation for the serious Bible student. Astonishingly, however, Jesus also said that He would prefer to have them **COLD instead of lukewarm! WHY WOULD JESUS, WHO COMMANDED EVERYONE TO "ENTER THROUGH THE NARROW GATE" (Matt. 7:13,14), MAKE SUCH AN ALARMING STATEMENT?** Could it be that if they were "cold" their example would **NOT** adversely affect so many with their indifference and apathy. Moreover, it would be easier for one who is "cold" to see their need for repentance than one who is "lukewarm." Perhaps Jesus was, therefore, thinking about their influence on others as well as their own welfare.

The love of the Lord Jesus is amazing. In Rev. 3:19, we see that Jesus **LOVES** the lukewarm Christian, **a worse condition that being "cold"!** Jesus' love for the lukewarm will, however, cause Him to **"REBUKE and DISCIPLINE"** them (verse 19)! **This clearly shows that SOME, but not all, of the adverse things that happen to Christians, especially the lukewarm ones, are sent**

directly from God to get them to draw closer to Him! Heb. 12:11 says, "No discipline seems pleasant at the time, **but PAINFUL.** Later on, however, **it produces a harvest of righteousness and peace for those who have been TRAINED by it."** Furthermore, **ALL CHRISTIANS** undergo God's discipline, **not just the lukewarm** (Heb. 12:7,8)! Jesus **WILL** subject the half-hearted to a "rebuke," then to "discipline" **FOR THEIR OWN GOOD.** Prov. 15:10 says, "Stern discipline awaits him who leaves the path...." The rebuke for the Laodiceans was probably issued at the reading of Rev. 3:14-22. There is no way of telling what the Lord's discipline for them was! We do, however, know that God "disciplined" the Israelites by sending them into exile (Isa. 26:13-16) and also when they were in the desert for forty years (Deut. 8:2-5). **IF** the lukewarm respond by drawing closer to God, seemingly they will do so only by **rebuke and discipline.** (Unfortunately, **SOME** won't respond, even to discipline, Jer. 17:23!) **The future for all the lukewarm is: first a rebuke, then discipline, then being expelled from the Body of Christ, if they still choose not to "be earnest and repent," verse 19.**

How much will God put up with before He spits the lukewarm out of the Body of Christ, or "cuts off" the person in Christ that bears no fruit (Jn. 15:2)? A definite answer from Scripture cannot be given. It must vary from individual to individual depending upon spiritual maturity and how often and severely God has already dealt with the individual about his/her rebellion. **Two things are certain: First, God is trying to keep us in the Body and on the vine - He's not trying to kick us out of His family, but keep us in His family! Secondly, if we persist in disobedience, God will honor our free will and let us go to our own spiritual death and the lake of the fire.**

We can also conclude that one can be "lukewarm" and still be saved FOR A TIME, as was the case with the Laodiceans. They were saved at the issuing of the Rev. 3:14-22 warning, but that would change if they wouldn't change.

Jesus said, "To him who overcomes, I will give the right to sit with me on my throne, just as I overcame and sat down with my Father on his throne," Rev. 3:21. **The context would tell us that He was speaking of OVERCOMING LUKEWARMNESS, which is still a problem today, as it was then.**

11

* Hell and Who Goes There *

The Bible says, "The LORD is COMPASSIONATE and GRACIOUS, SLOW TO ANGER, ABOUNDING IN LOVE" (Psa. 103:8). We should all rejoice in this fact about God, while we SERVE HIM WITH FEAR (Psa. 2:11). Yet there is another side of Him that many refuse to acknowledge, that is, **"The LORD is a JEALOUS AND AVENGING GOD; the LORD TAKES VENGEANCE and is <u>FILLED WITH WRATH</u>. The LORD TAKES VENGEANCE ON HIS FOES and <u>MAINTAINS</u> HIS WRATH AGAINST HIS ENEMIES. The LORD is SLOW TO ANGER and GREAT IN POWER; The LORD <u>WILL NOT</u> LEAVE THE GUILTY UNPUNISHED,"** Nah. 1:2,3.

In the New Testament, Paul wrote, **"But for those who are SELF-SEEKING and WHO REJECT THE TRUTH and FOLLOW EVIL, there <u>WILL BE</u> WRATH AND ANGER. There <u>WILL BE</u> TROUBLE AND DISTRESS for every human being WHO DOES EVIL..."** (Rom. 2:8,9). In other words, the unsaved will face **an ANGRY God** "FILLED WITH WRATH," then **ETERNAL** "TROUBLE AND DISTRESS" will be their inheritance. They will experience this special, God-designed **FIRE that is ETERNAL** (Matt. 18:8), **UNQUENCHABLE** (Mk. 9:48; Lk. 3:17) and **RAGING** (Heb. 10:27), that He directly prepared for the devil and his angels.

Perhaps the MOST TERRIFYING truth about the lake of fire is that it is **<u>FOREVER</u>**! There will be **NO HOPE** for those who go there - NO REPRIEVE! **It will seem like an unending nightmare for them.** After suffering 10,000 years, the lost will still have JUST AS LONG to suffer in this horrible place!

To cite only one argument to prove that there will be NO ANNIHILATION FOR THE WICKED, please notice Rev. 20:

10, "And the devil, who deceived them, was thrown into the lake of burning sulfur, where the beast and the false prophet **had been thrown. They will be TORMENTED DAY AND NIGHT FOR**

"TORMENTED DAY AND NIGHT FOR EVER AND EVER"

EVER AND EVER." According to Rev. 19:20, the beast and the false prophet were thrown into "the FIERY lake of burning sulfur" BEFORE the Millennium! **This means that for at least 1,000 years, yet in the future, these two men will be tormented in this unusual fire WITHOUT BEING ANNIHILATED!** Furthermore, those men will be thrown into this "fiery lake" with the kind of bodies we have now! [This clearly proves that that fire is not the kind of fire we are familiar with, for if it was, their bodies would be burnt to ashes in just a fraction of that time. Also, since the devil is a spirit and he will be tormented by this fire, it can't be the kind of fire we are accustomed to. In other words, the fire God has in store for the wicked can torment spirits!] Their torment will **NEVER** cease in the final place for them, the lake of fire.

Those who go there will **NEVER** hear a kind word, **NEVER** see a kind look and **NEVER** observe a kind act. Besides the sincere-but-religiously-deceived, **the worst kind of people THAT EVER LIVED will be there** - homosexuals, child molesters, rapists, adulterers, murderers, drunkards, thieves, devil worshippers, idolaters, the greedy, the jealous, the unforgiving, the church hypocrite, the lustful, the liars and the like who did not "deny themselves, take up their cross daily and follow me [Jesus]," Lk. 9:23. See Matt. 5:28,29; Matt. 6:14,15; 1 Cor. 6:9-11; Gal. 5:19-21; Eph. 5:5-7; Rev. 21:8; Rev. 22:15. The continual sounds heard there will be PLEADING FOR MERCY, WEEPING, CURSING GOD and AGONIZING GROANS CAUSED BY THEIR PAIN. This will be their lot **FOREVER**, because they chose to be SELF-SEEKING, REJECT THE TRUTH and FOLLOW EVIL (Rom. 2:8) during their time of testing in this life.

"RAGING" is a word used to describe forest fires that are completely out of control. In 1988 such a fire was loose at Yellowstone National Park. The flames were reported as being 300 feet high! Likewise, the flames that torment in the lake of fire are "RAGING," that is VIOLENT and INTENSE. **Billions of humans and possibly quadrillions of demons will co-exist there**

FOREVER IN TORMENT!

ALL who spend their eternity in the lake of burning sulfur will be "**THROWN**" into it - the devil (Rev. 20:10), the antichrist and false prophet (Rev. 19:20) and all other humans who died unsaved (Matt. 13:42; Rev. 20:15). BILLIONS of people will be THROWN into these fires. Many that we personally know and some we PRESENTLY GO TO CHURCH WITH will be of this number! **"SHAME AND EVERLASTING CONTEMPT" (Dan. 12:2) is in their future also, besides being FORGOTTEN BY THEIR FAMILIES AND FRIENDS WHO GO TO HEAVEN (Isa. 65:17).** The damned will think about God FOREVER then, though now, in this present life, some "think it not worthy to retain the knowledge of God," Rom. 1:28. All people in Hell exhibited goat-like rebellion to His will (Matt. 25:31-46; Lk. 19:27). They will experience this "**FIERY FURNACE**" the Lord said exists (Matt. 13:42,50) and the "**BLACKEST DARKNESS**" that both Peter and Jude wrote of (2 Pet. 2:17; Jude 13). Hell will be NO PARTY, according to the Bible! Some who refuse to REPENT and TRUST JESUS 100% for their soul's salvation say, "I'll take my chances." But they really aren't! It's a SURE THING that they will be THROWN INTO THIS LAKE. There is NO CHANCE they will escape (Lk. 13:3; Jn. 14:6; Acts 4:12)!

Perhaps for those who were once saved, then "fall away" (Lk. 8:13) or are "disowned" by Christ (Matt. 10:33) or become "dead" as the Prodigal (Lk. 15:24,32) or "believed in vain" (1 Cor. 15:2) or "have fallen away from grace" (Gal. 5:4) or RETURNED TO THEIR FORMER LIFESTYLE OF SINNING AFTER HAVING ESCAPED THE CORRUPTION OF THE WORLD BY KNOWING JESUS CHRIST (2 Pet. 2:20-22), this place we call "Hell" will be MOST HORRIBLE. (This is assuming that such a person does NOT come back to the Lord as Peter did after he disowned

THOUGH PAINFUL TO ADMIT, YOU POTENTIALLY CAN STILL GO TO HELL, EVEN IF YOU ARE A CHRISTIAN AT THIS MOMENT!

Christ.) According to Jesus, five out of ten who were once saved, in the last generation, will experience this fate (Matt. 25:1-13)! THOUGH PAINFUL TO ADMIT, YOU POTENTIALLY CAN STILL GO TO HELL, EVEN IF YOU ARE A CHRISTIAN AT

THIS MOMENT! To believe otherwise is to be deceived about the Biblical record!

As HORRIBLE as the lake of fire is, Heaven is GOOD! See Isa. 35:10; Rom. 2:10; Rev. 21:4; etc. There will be no death, mourning, crying, pain, curse, night or devil, while the overcomers reign with God there! This paradise environment where joy and music abides is, however, reserved ONLY for the redeemed, that is, **those who DENIED THEMSELVES, TOOK UP THEIR CROSS DAILY and FOLLOWED JESUS UNASHAMEDLY (Lk. 9:23-26).** The same group is labeled "**worthy**" in Rev. 3:4-6, "Yet you have a few people in Sardis who have not soiled their clothes. They will walk with me, dressed in white, for they are **worthy**. He who **overcomes** will, like them, be dressed in white. **I will never erase his name from the book of life**, but will acknowledge his name before my Father and his angels. He who has an ear, let him hear what the Spirit says to the churches." Furthermore, Jesus said, "Anyone who loves his father or mother more than me is **NOT WORTHY OF ME**; anyone who loves his son or daughter more than me is **NOT WORTHY OF ME**; and anyone who does not take his cross and follow me is **NOT WORTHY OF ME**. Whoever finds his life **WILL LOSE IT**, and whoever loses his life for my sake will find it," Matt. 10:37-39.

12

* Safeguards For You *

In the Parable of the Ten Virgins, Jesus taught that five out of ten (or **50%**) of the people that had a fire burning for God at one time will NOT be known by Him when He returns! See Matt. 25:1-13. THIS REFERS TO THE LAST GENERATION. This same incredible apostasy-warning is also found in Matt. 24:10; 2 Thess. 2:3; 1 Tim. 4:1 and 2 Tim. 4:4. It's eternally important, therefore, that we are not like the "foolish" virgins of Matt. 25:1-13! If they would have only brought some extra oil, their future would have been different. This is where YOU and "safeguards" come in!

Spiritual **SAFEGUARDS** are real, very important and should be taken seriously. Listed are seventeen safeguards for your spiritual health and well being. The more of these you act upon, the more you will benefit.

Phil. 3:1 reads, "Finally, my brothers, rejoice in the Lord! It is no trouble for me to write the same thing to you again, and it is a **SAFEGUARD for you.**"

1 REJOICE IN THE LORD. Because the Christians at Philippi were going through (and enduring) sufferings and struggles (Phil. 1:29,30), Paul issued the command (safeguard) for them to "REJOICE IN THE LORD."

Similarly, Jesus told the disciples, "However, do not rejoice that the spirits submit to you, but rejoice that your names are written in heaven," Lk. 10:20. What an incredible, but real and glorious future you have as a Christian beyond the grave. In 2 Cor. 9:15, eternal life is called an "indescribable gift."

Also remember that **NO Christian ever had it ideal in this life! You are not alone with your troubles and sufferings (Jn. 16:33; 1 Pet. 5:9)**. You are living in a cursed age, with rampant deception, sin and injustice everywhere. Also, this world is now the devil's turf and he hates Christians. Obviously, this world isn't the saint's haven. Paul wrote, "For our light and momentary troubles are achieving for us an eternal glory that **far outweighs them all**. So we fix our eyes not on what is seen, but on what is unseen. For **what is seen is temporary**, but what is unseen is eternal," 2 Cor. 4:17,18.

2 **BE HUMBLE AND STAY HUMBLE** like a little child. Jesus shockingly warned **his disciples** that they would never enter the kingdom of heaven unless they would change and become HUMBLE like little children **(Matt. 18:1-4)**! In other words, though they were saved at the moment, their selfish ambition to be greater than the other disciples (Lk. 9:46-48; 22:24-26) would prove spiritually fatal in the future for them; that is, they would not stay saved and enter the kingdom of heaven in the end, unless they would become HUMBLE like a little child, who doesn't aspire for such greatness over his peers the way they were!

Peter later wrote, "Clothe yourselves with HUMILITY toward one another, because 'God opposes the proud but gives grace to the HUMBLE.' HUMBLE YOURSELVES, therefore, under God's mighty hand, that he may lift you up in due time," 1 Pet. 5:5,6. Verse 6 from the Amplified Bible reads, "Therefore humble yourselves (demote, lower yourselves in your own estimation) under the mighty hand of God, that in due time He may exalt you." See also Jam. 4:6.

3 **HIDE GOD'S WORD IN YOUR HEART**. Psa. 119:11 says, "I have hidden your word in my heart that I might not sin against you." To strengthen your own ability to resist sin's temptations, store up God's word in your heart! You can accomplish this by MEDITATING IN and MEMORIZING SCRIP-

TURE. One method that might work well for you is to make little flash cards with the Scripture verse you desire to memorize on one side and its reference on the reverse side. Verbally reading the verse/s out loud and writing them out will enable you to memorize almost any passage after a while. It would also be wise to listen to the Bible on cassette tape every chance you get, such as in your home and car.

4 **STAY FULLY COMMITTED TO GOD** and 2 Chron. 16:9 will apply to you: "For the eyes of the LORD range throughout the earth to strengthen those whose hearts are fully committed to him...." It's one thing to "build yourself up" (Jude 20), but it's totally different to be strengthened by God!

5 **DO NOT EVEN THINK ABOUT THE "PLEASURES OF SIN" (Heb. 11:25).** Heb. 11:15,16 say, "If they had been thinking of the country they had left, **they would have had opportunity to return**. Instead, they were longing for a better country - a heavenly one. Therefore God is not ashamed to be called their God, for he has prepared a city for them."

Remember the awesome truth of Num. 11:5 where this is exemplified, that is, the Israelites thought about the fish, cucumbers, melons, leeks, onions and garlic that they regularly ate while in bondage in Egypt (a type of the world), but couldn't find contentment with their God-supplied food, manna. Because they focused in upon the good things while in Egypt, they had totally forgotten that they were worked ruthlessly and their lives were made bitter with hard labor (Ex. 1:13,14)! The misery and emptiness of their lives in Egypt had escaped them! They now, incredibly, thought they were better off in Egypt (Num. 11:18)!

We should always be looking FORWARD and never back. Peter wrote: "...We are looking **forward** to a new heaven and a new earth, the home of righteousness (2 Pet. 3:13). Similarly, Heb. 13:14 reads, "For here we do not have an enduring city, but **we are looking for** the city that is to come."

If you follow this principle you won't disobey Rom. 13:14b, "...Do not think about how to gratify the desires of the sinful nature." To avoid watching adulterous TV shows and places such as public swimming pools and beaches will definitely be a safeguard for your soul! See Matt. 5:28. **Also, ponder the truth about how your thought life influences your behavior (Rom. 8:5,6).**

6 CONSIDER JESUS, so you won't grow weary and lose heart in your race. Heb. 12:3,4: "Consider him who endured such opposition from sinful men, so that you will not grow weary and lose heart. In your struggle against sin, you have not yet resisted to the point of shedding your blood." The word "consider" in Greek means CONTEMPLATE. Therefore, **we are advised to CONTEMPLATE the unfair, unjust and merciless treatment the perfect and sinless Lord Jesus was subjected to.** He didn't deserve any of it. (This would be an excellent Bible study for you to do.)

7 LEARN THE BIBLE. This is the all-inclusive safeguard. Hos. 4:6 reads, "My people are destroyed from lack of knowledge." The ONLY way you can learn the Bible is to spend **quality time in it for yourself.** Start in the New Testament, reading and rereading it so that no zealous and sincere false prophet or false teacher can shake the true message from your heart. After you learn the New Testament, move to the Old Testament. The Old Testament was written to "teach" and "warn" us in New Testament times (Rom. 15:4; 1 Cor. 10:11). It was also the ONLY Bible the earliest Christians had before the New Testament was written! There is much in it for you.

Witnessing to others about Christ will add to your understanding of spiritual things: "I pray that you may be active in sharing your faith, so that you will have a full understanding of every good thing we have in Christ," Philemon 6.

A good, reliable, easy-to-read translation like the New International Version or the New King James will help you greatly in learning the Bible.

8 DO NOT ENVY THE UNSAVED. Read Psalm 73. Asaph envied the wicked and "almost slipped" spiritually. He noticed the prosperity they have, their healthy bodies, them being carefree and free from burdens common to man and not plagued by human ills and he thought "in vain have I kept my heart pure; in vain have I washed my hands in innocence," verse 13. Asaph was oppressed until he focused in upon their "final destiny" (v.17).

Don't envy the wicked because they might be popular, happily married, with a good job, physically healthy, good looking, live in a nice home, drive a new car and have lots of money. **They are on their way to the lake of fire where they will be TORMENTED FOREVER (Matt. 25:41,46; Mk. 9:43-48; Rev. 14:10,11; 20:10).** To envy the wicked is a subtle Satanic temptation designed to get you to stop living godly and to pursue the temporal pleasures of this life.

9 **MAINTAIN A BIBLICAL VIEW OF PHYSICAL DEATH AND YOUR LIFE HERE.** This will be especially helpful in extreme persecution, where martyrdom prevails.

For the Christian, physical death is "**gain**" (Phil. 1:21) and "**better by far**" (Phil. 1:23). Only then will you really be at "home" with your real family, that is, your Heavenly Father, your Lord and Savior Jesus Christ, and your brothers and sisters in the faith from all parts of the earth. It's also where your treasures are. This life is not your home! We are "strangers in the world" (1 Pet. 1:1) and we are to live our lives "as strangers here in reverent fear" (1 Pet. 1:17). You are just passing through this life, so don't be engrossed in the material things of this world! Think in terms of eternity. Remember, "...The heavens will disappear with a roar; the elements will be destroyed by fire, and **the earth and everything in it will be laid bare**" (2 Pet. 3:10).

10 **MAINTAIN THE HOPE OF BEING LIKE JESUS WHEN HE RETURNS.** 1 Jn. 3:2,3 read: "Dear friends, now we are children of God, and what we will be has not yet been made known. But we know that when he appears, we shall be like him, for we shall see him as he is. **Everyone who has this hope in him purifies himself, just as he is pure.**"

How will we be like Jesus? We too will have a glorified body of flesh and bones like his (Lk. 24:39; Phil. 3:21), that is, a tangible body that can enter a room with the doors locked (Jn. 20:19) and disappear from a location (Lk. 24:31).

11 **PRAY TO STAND FIRM IN ALL THE WILL OF GOD.** In Col. 4:12, we read, "...He (Epaphras) is always wrestling in prayer for you, that you may stand firm in all the will of God, mature and fully assured." Be quick to pray about everything you face, casting all your anxieties on God (1 Pet. 5:7). Pray for other people, too.

12 **BE FILLED WITH THE SPIRIT.** Eph. 5:18-20 read, "...Be filled with the Spirit. Speak to one another with psalms, hymns and spiritual songs. Sing and make music

in your heart to the Lord, always giving thanks to God the Father for everything, in the name of our Lord Jesus Christ." To keep a godly tune in your heart will help you greatly in your spiritual battles, as will maintaining a thankful attitude for what you do have and what God has done for you. **Focus in upon what you have, NOT what you do not have but would like to have!** In other words, learn to be **CONTENT** in your non-ideal circumstances. This is a "safe-guard" in itself. Paul wrote, "I have learned to be **CONTENT** whatever the circumstances" (Phil. 4:11). Remember, he was in chains and in prison when he wrote this (1:13)! Furthermore, he wrote, "But **godliness with CONTENTMENT** is great gain. For we brought nothing into the world, and we can take nothing out of it. But **if we have food and clothing, we will be CONTENT with that**" (1 Tim. 6:6-8).

13 AVOID GODLESS CHATTER. 2 Tim. 2:16 reads, "**Avoid godless chatter, because those who indulge in it will become more and more ungodly.**" Secular TV shows are prime examples of godless chatter! Furthermore, they promote a value system which is usually highly antithetical to the Scriptures.

Also, indulging in voluntary conversation on a regular basis with the darkened people of this age will take a spiritual toll after a while, that is, if spiritual matters are intentionally avoided by the spiritually enlightened. Similarly, Paul wrote in 1 Tim. 6:20, "...Turn away from godless chatter and the opposing ideas of what is falsely called knowledge, which some have professed and in so doing have **wandered from the faith.**" The danger of godless chatter is evident from this.

14 **STAY SELF-CONTROLLED, ALERT AND CONTINUE TO RESIST THE DEVIL.** This is the way we can protect ourselves from our spiritual enemy. "Be self-controlled and alert. **Your enemy the devil prowls around like a roaring lion LOOKING FOR SOMEONE TO DEVOUR.** Resist him, standing firm in the faith, because you know that your brothers throughout the world are undergoing the same kind of sufferings," 1 Pet. 5:8,9. The seriousness of this spiritual warfare is shown here.

15 **AVOID "BAD COMPANY."** Surprisingly, the Bible teaches that **Christians are to avoid certain people** (Prov. 20:19; 22:24,25; 24:1; Rom. 16:17,18; 1 Cor. 5:11; 2 Thess. 3:6-15), **places** (Prov. 4:14,15; 5:8; 2 Cor. 6:17) **and things** (Prov. 20:3; Acts 15:29; 1 Thess. 5:22; 2 Tim. 2:23; Jam. 1:19,20). Not to do so, when you can, is to needlessly open yourself up to spiritual danger. Paul wrote: "**Do NOT be misled: BAD COMPANY CORRUPTS GOOD CHARACTER**" (1 Cor. 15:33). Please note, according to that reference, bad company tends to adversely affect the Christian and not the reverse. This, however, does not mean that we willingly should never associate with the unbeliever, for we are called to evangelize them. **Jesus ate with the sinners, but He did so with an evangelistic motive only.**

Especially destructive to one's spiritual condition would be to marry someone that does not "belong to the Lord" (1 Cor. 7:39). This is evident by what happened to Solomon when he married pagan women. **See Neh. 13:26.** If you are a single Christian, please know that it is much worse to marry the wrong person than to remain single, though it can be painfully lonely at times!

16 **KNOW THAT PERSECUTION COMES TO ALL OF THE GODLY AND YOU MUST TESTIFY ABOUT JESUS.** In Jn. 16:1, Jesus said, "All **THIS** I have told you so that you will not **go astray.**" To find out what "this" is in this verse we must go back to chapter 15. There we will see the Lord assured the disciples that the world would hate and persecute them (15:18-20)! Furthermore, He added that we must "TESTIFY" of him. These two truths, internalized and acted upon, will keep us from going "astray," according to Jesus.

17 **FEAR GOD.** He's the only one that can destroy your soul in Hell (Matt. 10:28; Lk. 12:5). This command is PAST (Deut. 10:12,13), PRESENT (1 Pet. 1:17), and FUTURE (Rev. 14:7). While the fear of man will prove to be a snare (Prov. 29:25), only good can be said about the fear of God! **If you truly fear God, you will never backslide or turn from God (Jer. 32:40).** [We offer an important cassette tape on the fear of God. See the catalog of available cassettes, on a wide variety of subjects, in the back of this book.]

13

Summary

In spite of all the enclosed Biblical evidence, a portion of the people who read this study will continue to deny the obvious and cling tenaciously to the comfortable but false doctrine of U. E. S. to the destruction of others and maybe themselves as well! For some a **FALSE SECURITY**, which overlooks relevant warnings, is more important than the disturbing truth!

Others have never really thought these things out or heard the Scriptural reasons why so many don't believe in U. E. S. Understandably, they were swayed by popular, glib TV and radio teachers that will never share the Scriptures and rationale cited in this study. Such people need to carefully reread this entire book verifying every Scripture verse, checking the context and pondering every argument for themselves. Don't be wrongly swayed by the impressive title of "Dr." or the "Berean" claim by those that are U. E. S. adherents. Many carry these titles and claims! The Bible ALONE is the Christian's FINAL AUTHORITY (2 Tim. 3:16,17).

The only reason any Christian would believe in a conditional security for the believer is because the Bible teaches it! No one wants to believe in it on their own! It's just like the true, but horrifying, teaching that most people will perish and will experience eternal, conscious torment forever. No one wants to believe this apart from the Bible.

Our hope is that you, the reader, have a teachable heart that will submit to the Scriptures, though it may be disturbing, even painful!

Follow Jesus

There is a "secure position" in Christ, but it is one from which we can still "fall" (2 Pet. 3:17)! We must CONTINUE to follow Christ so that we will "never perish" (Jn. 10:27,28)!

Peter also said, "Be all the more eager to make your calling and election sure. For if you do these things, you will NEVER FALL..." (2 Pet. 1:10). Read verses 5-9 to find out what "these things" are. (This is another important safeguard.)

Yes, God will always do His part to protect us spiritually and He will never fail, but there is still free will and the human responsibilities. **WE CAN AND STILL DO INFLUENCE OUR OWN FUTURE WITH GOD EVEN INTO ETERNITY! OUR HEARTS CAN "TURN AWAY" FROM GOD** as Solomon's heart did (1 Ki. 11:9)! Frightening but true, Solomon's heart turned from God to idolatry after decades of faithful service! THE SAME CAN HAPPEN TO US, if we don't guard our hearts. Jesus was not exaggerating when He said, "Make every effort to enter through the narrow door, because many, I tell you, will try to enter and will not be able to" (Lk. 13:24). The Greek shows that He said, "**KEEP MAKING EVERY EFFORT.**" Also, the Greek word is the one from which we get our word "**agonize**"! In other words, don't ever stop **agonizing** in spiritual battle till you actually enter the kingdom of God! The doctrine of U. E. S. gives Christian people a false and dangerous sense of security that removes the Lord's sound advice of Lk. 13:24 far from the heart! A prime example of this is what Charles Stanley said:

> *"How do you stay saved? What do you do to stay saved? Nothing! Absolutely nothing! You say, 'Suppose I stop believing.' I'm going to show you in a minute that you can't do it! I'm going to show you, you can't stop believing. If you've been saved by the grace of God, you cannot stop believing!"* [33]

Another example of this comes from J. Vernon McGee, a deceased U. E. S. teacher, who promoted the opposite of Lk. 13:24:

> *"He* [God] *never lets go. Now sit back, relax, and enjoy your salvation."* [34]

Though dead, McGee's teachings are audibly heard from past recordings over the radio program, Thru The Bible.

Remember these important points spoken by Jesus: First, "And from the days of John the Baptist until the present time the kingdom of heaven has endured violent assault, and violent men seize it by force [as a precious prize] - a share in the heavenly kingdom **is sought for with most ardent zeal and intense exertion**" (Matt. 11:12, Amplified Bible).

Second, "And He said to all, If any person wills to come after Me, let him deny himself - that is, disown himself, forget, lose sight of himself and his own interests, refuse and give up himself -

and take up his cross **DAILY**, and follow Me [that is, cleave steadfastly to Me, conform wholly to My example, in living and if need be in dying also]" (Lk. 9:23, Amplified Bible).

Third, "But seek first His kingdom and His righteousness..." (Matt. 6:33). The Greek shows this is a continuous tense, that is, Jesus said **KEEP SEEKING FIRST** HIS KINGDOM AND HIS RIGHTEOUSNESS.

Finally, Jesus said, "**DIFFICULT** is the way which leads to life" (Matt. 7:14, N.K.J.V.). The N.R.S.V. renders this same verse, "The road is **HARD** that leads to life."

If you are a teacher, remember you are NOT in a popularity contest (1 Thess. 2:4)! Your aim should be to please God and win His approval (Gal. 1:10)! Your judgment as a teacher will be MORE STRICT than others (Jam. 3:1). **Do NOT, therefore, compromise the truth of Scripture to please your audience or to promote your own ministry.** Jesus never did. Many walked away from Him and His message to never return, by no fault of His! **The truth is vital**, though it might be hard to receive at times and hard to give out, especially when you know in advance that some will be unhappy with it! **Such is one of the hardest tests a faithful minister will ever face.** For the sake of eternal souls and your own judgment on that awesome Day, take to heart God's advice given through Paul - "**Herald and preach the Word!** Keep your sense of urgency (stand by, be at hand and ready, **whether the opportunity seems to be favorable or unfavorable, whether it is convenient or inconvenient, whether it is welcome or unwelcome**, you as a preacher of the Word are to **show people in what way their lives are wrong) and convince them, rebuking and correcting, warning and urging and encouraging them, being unflagging and inexhaustible in patience and teaching.** For the time is coming when [people] will **not tolerate (endure) sound and wholesome instruction, but having ears itching [for something pleasing and gratifying]**, they will gather to themselves one teacher after another to a considerable number, chosen to **satisfy their own liking and to foster the errors they hold**, and will turn aside from hearing the truth and **wander off into myths and man-made fictions**" (2 Tim. 4:2-4, Amplified Bible). Paul told us "the time is coming" when people will not tolerate (endure) sound and wholesome instruction. **THAT TIME HAS COME! IT IS NO LONGER FUTURISTIC, BUT PRESENT TENSE! Make it your goal to PLEASE GOD, not the people with "itching ears" whom you know in advance will seek out many teachers to accommodate their wishes doctrinally!**

The truth of God, especially regarding salvation, is always worth being "divisive" over, as Paul publicly demonstrated (Gal. 2:11-14). Don't let being labeled "divisive," as some accuse, stop you from boldly speaking out and openly refuting the MYTH of eternal security in our day! Remember Judgment Day!

How could any subject from the Bible, so closely linked to the gospel (1 Cor. 15:2; Col. 1:23) and associated with one inheriting the kingdom of God or not (Gal. 5:19-21) be a "non-essential," as some say? Yet if one disagrees with their myth, he is labeled "divisive" over a non-essential subject!

If you are a pastor, you are not a very good shepherd, to say the least, if you know U. E. S. is wrong and you are afraid to publicly express it to your congregation; especially in light of all the U. E. S. messages pouring out over the airwaves and found in literature. **The U. E. S. teachers aren't afraid to teach their harmful myths with conviction and authority!**

Remember this, Adrian Rogers, a U. E. S. teacher, was so bold as to say in one of his sermons that eternal security is "*fundamental,*" "*necessary for your spiritual health*" and one is a spiritual "*neurotic*" unless he believes in this teaching![35] Another U. E. S. author went so far as to write in one of his books:

> "*The eternal security of the believer arises out of the necessity and nature of the atonement.*" [36]

(In spite of Robert Morey's statement quoted here, we highly recommend his numerous books and his radio broadcast, Truth Seekers, which are both insightful and informative.)

UNCONDITIONAL ETERNAL SECURITY NEEDS TO BE BOLDLY ADDRESSED AND REFUTED AS NEVER BEFORE!

Unfortunately, these types of statements are not isolated ones! To reiterate, three different U. E. S. teachers previously quoted have stated: promoters of false religion reject U. E. S., concluded those who differ with them have "*another Jesus,*" teach "*salvation by works*" and don't understand what it means to believe on Christ!

UNCONDITIONAL ETERNAL SECURITY NEEDS TO BE BOLDLY ADDRESSED AND REFUTED AS NEVER BEFORE! Remember, if you are a pastor, you are to "keep watch over" the ones God has entrusted into your care (Heb. 13:17). Also, let the words of 1 Tim. 4:16 remain with you, "**Watch your life and DOCTRINE closely. Persevere in them, because if you do, you will save both yourself and your hearers.**"

Everyone needs to remember Jam. 1:12: "Blessed is the man who **PERSEVERES** under trial, because when he has stood the **TEST**, he will receive the crown of life that God has promised to those who love him." (The important question is **DO WE LOVE GOD** not DOES HE LOVE US!) To get the "crown of life" that James speaks of we MUST persevere through our many TESTS now, which will indicate that we love God. (Please note this life is now a time of testing for us all, not a time of "enjoying God" as many seem to strive for.)

Let Jam. 5:19,20 motivate YOU: "My brothers, if one of you should **wander from the truth** and someone should bring him back, remember this: Whoever turns a sinner from the error of his way will **save him from death** and cover over a multitude of sins." (Perhaps this book will help in this endeavor.) U. E. S. proponents usually interpret "death" here and in many other similar places as being physical. However, this surely cannot be anything but spiritual death. Remember, **the Prodigal Son did not die physically when he was living in constant immorality, when his spiritual condition degenerated from ALIVE to DEAD!** Some U. E. S. proponents believe God will kill a person physically, before he/she will die spiritually because of unrepented, unconfessed sin. [This is their interpretation of the "sin that leads to death" (1 Jn. 5:16).] This too is a false security in itself, as shown by David, Solomon, the Prodigal Son, Demas, Judas and others already mentioned.

Some of the U. E. S. teachers **with great influence** in our day, though all aren't still living, are: John R. Rice, Jack Van Impe, Dave Breese, Hal Lindsey, Charles Stanley, Cal Beisner, John MacArthur, Jr., Fritz Ridenour, Dave Hunt, J. Vernon McGee, Adrian Rogers, R. C. Sproul, D. James Kennedy, Bob George, Charles Swindoll, Charles Ryrie, Bob Larson, Jerry Falwell, Hank Hanegraaff, Robert Morey, Hugh Pyle, Bill Jackson, John Ankerberg, John Weldon, James Montgomery Boice, Ron Rhodes, Marvin Rosenthal, David Levy and H. A. Ironside.

Though these men hold to many sound teachings, yet they embrace U. E. S. (John Ankerberg, Dave Hunt and Robert Morey, especially, have done much good in the field of general apologetics. Also, Bill Jackson needs to be commended for his courage and love for Catholics, as he devotes his time and energy in ministry in helping them find salvation.)

The majority of Biblical references cited in this study are from the New International Version. If you accept the 1611 King James Version only, please take the time to verify all references with that version. DO NOT DISREGARD THIS STUDY OVER THAT POINT!

For additional copies of this book, please send in **only $5.00 per copy plus 15% of your total order for postage and packaging. (In other words, send only $5.75 for one copy.) THIS IS A 44% DISCOUNT OFF THE SUGGESTED RETAIL PRICE TO HELP GET THIS MUCH-NEEDED MESSAGE OUT!** If you can't afford the full price, send what you can and you will receive one copy. If you purchase 10 or more copies of this book for distribution to others, the price is reduced to $4.00 per copy plus 15% of your total order for postage and packaging. Make your personal check or money order in U.S. funds payable to EVANGELICAL OUTREACH and mail to:

EVANGELICAL OUTREACH
P. O. BOX 265
WASHINGTON, PA 15301-0265

Your questions, comments, and/or criticisms are welcome.

SEMINARS on unconditional eternal security, evangelism, revival services, and/or various false religious systems are available and can be scheduled for your church or group. Write to the above address or phone (412) 632-6740.

GOD BLESS YOU.

"Test everything. Hold on to the good. Avoid every kind of evil" (1 Thess. 5:21,22).

* Notes *

1 Ron Rhodes, Reasoning From The Scriptures With The Jehovah's Witnesses, Harvest House Publishers, 1993, pp.302,303.
2 Jack Van Impe, Escape The Second Death, Jack Van Impe Ministries, 1985, p.23.
3 John R. Rice, Eternal Salvation, Sword Of The Lord Publishers, 1973, back cover.
4 Dave Breese, Know the Marks of Cults, Victor Books, 1978, p.43.
5 David Levy, Israel My Glory, October/November 1993, Vol.51, No.5, "Victorious Christian Living," p.25.
6 Hal Lindsey, Satan Is Alive And Well On Planet Earth, Zondervan Publishing House, 1972, pp.193,194.
7 John R. Rice, Can A Saved Person Ever Be Lost?, Sword Of The Lord Publishers, 1943, p.16.
8 Charles Stanley, Saved And Sure, (cassette tape #AW114).
9 Cal Beisner, tract: Can The Believer Lose His Salvation?, Christian Research Institute, 1979, p.2.
10 John R. Rice, Can A Saved Person Ever Be Lost?, Sword Of The Lord Publishers, 1943, p.8.
11 John MacArthur, Jr., Our Sufficiency In Christ, Word Publishing, 1991, p.51.
12 David N. Steele and Curtis C. Thomas, The Five Points Of Calvinism, Presbyterian & Reformed Publishing Co., 1984, p.56.
13 Cal Beisner, Is Baptism Necessary For Salvation?, Christian Apologetics: Research and Information Service, 1980, Conclusion.
14 The NIV Study Bible, New International Version, Zondervan Bible Publishers, 1985 edition, p.1554.
15 The Ryrie Study Bible, (Chicago: Moody Press, 1986), p.1614.
16 John R. Rice, Can A Saved Person Ever Be Lost?, Sword Of The Lord Publishers, 1943, p.13.
17 Robert Young, Young's Analytical Concordance To The Bible, Eerdmans Publishing Company, 1973, p.245.
18 Stanley Toussaint, tract: Can a Believer Lose His Salvation? The Good News Broadcasting Association, Inc., 1979, p.2.
19 D. James Kennedy, The Perseverance of the Saints (pamphlet), Coral Ridge Ministries, p.5.
20 Jack Hayford, The Sin of Suicide, (Cassette Tape #CO124, tape 1).
21 James Montgomery Boice, "Bible Answer Man" Radio Talk Show, 11/2/93.
22 D. James Kennedy, The Perseverance of the Saints (pamphlet), Coral Ridge Ministries, p.9.
23 Myer Pearlman, Knowing The Doctrines Of The Bible, Gospel Publishing House, 1937, pp.271,272.
24 Bob George, "People To People" Radio Talk Show, 11/9/93.
25 ibid., 11/16/93.
26 John R. Rice, Can A Saved Person Ever Be Lost?, Sword Of The Lord Publishers, 1943, p.21.
27 Hank Hanegraaff, CRI Perspective, Christians And The Assurance Of Salvation.
28 Dave Hunt, CIB Bulletin, Christian Information Bureau, June 1989, Vol.5, No.6, p.1.
29 ibid.
30 ibid.
31 Earl Paulk, Satan Unmasked (Atlanta: K Dimension Publishers, 1984), p.96.
32 Fritz Ridenour, So What's The Difference?, Regal Books, 1984, pp.44,45.
33 Charles Stanley, Saved And Sure, (cassette tape #AW114).
34 J. Vernon McGee, How You Can Have The Assurance Of Salvation, Seth's Printing, 1976, p.12.
35 Adrian Rogers, How You Can Be Sure You Are Eternally Secure-Part 1, Jn. 10:27 (Cassette Tape #RA-1728), 8-1-93A.
36 Robert A. Morey, The Saving Work of Christ, T/A GAM Printers, 1980, p.235.

✻ Scripture Index ✻

* Subject Index *

A VIVID, CLEAR PRESENTATION USING OVERHEAD TRANSPARENCIES AND SHOCKING AUDIO RECORDINGS SUCH AS THE FOLLOWING:

"And as Paul said, 'All things are permissible, but not all things are profitable.' SO IS COMMITTING FORNICATION PERMISSIBLE? YES. Is it profitable? No, it isn't."

The general command to "contend for the faith" is still very relevant in our day (Jude 3). As Jude went on to say, certain men have "change[d] the grace of our God into a license for immorality..." (v.4) as the above quote shows!

SEMINARS

ON THE BELIEVER'S SECURITY,
THE TRUE AND THE FALSE,
ARE AVAILABLE BY CONTACTING:

EVANGELICAL OUTREACH
P. O. BOX 265
WASHINGTON, PA 15301
(412) 632-6740

⁎ Catalog of Literature and Cassettes ⁎

PRICES EFFECTIVE 3/1/94 THROUGH 3/1/96

LITERATURE

Packet of literature for Jehovah's Witnesses	*$1.00*
Packet of literature for Mormons	*1.00*
Packet of literature for Catholics	*1.00*
Packet of literature for Masons	*1.00*
Study refuting baptismal regeneration	*.50*
Tract for Saturday Sabbatarians	*.10*
Answering the Most Common Objections to the Deity of Christ	*.10*
Questions for Teachable Unconditional Eternal Security Proponents	*.10*
25 or more of the above questionnaires	*.07*
Open Letter to Charles Stanley	*.05*
"Evolution versus creation" tract	*FREE*

ALL THE FOLLOWING CASSETTE MESSAGES ARE JUST $3.00 EACH

[For every 4 tapes you purchase, you get one __FREE__ tape.] If you purchase 20 tapes, you get 8 __FREE__ tapes. (If you sincerely cannot afford the cost of these tapes, but would like to hear them, any two tapes will be sent absolutely __FREE__.)

__Orders under $20.00__: Include $2.00 for postage and packaging; __orders over $20.00__: Include 10% of total for postage and packaging.

CASSETTE MESSAGES BY DAN CORNER

A Man Highly Esteemed by God
Almost a Backslider
Anger-the Good and the Bad
Answering Objections to the Deity of Christ
Ashamed or Not Ashamed-God Knows the Heart
Avoid Every Kind of Evil
Be Ready
Bible Study Methods, I*
Bible Study Methods, II
Bible Study Methods, III
Bible Verses That Some Christians Do Not Believe!
Biblical Grace
Caught in a Storm
Christ's Ambassadors in the World
Christian Singleness
Demons, According to the Bible
Distinguishing God's Truth From Error
Evidence of Saving Grace
Examining the Charismatic Conference and the Ecumenical Movement
False Prophets of Our Day, I
False Prophets of Our Day, II
God's Invisible Army
Guilt, the Real and the False
How to Study Your Bible, I
How to Study Your Bible, II
How to Study Your Bible, III
I Will Make You Fishers of Men
"It is Mine to Avenge, I Will Repay," says the Lord
Jehovah's Witnesses, Witnessing to
Jesus' Reliance on Prayer
Josiah, the Mighty Reformer
Jude's Final Written Words
Lukewarmness
Let's Go Back
Lying, the Nature of Satan and the Old Self
Make Every Effort To
Money and the Related
Mormonism, The Truth About
New Testament Warnings
Not Everyone Who Says to Me, 'Lord, Lord'
Paradise Restored
Paul at Berea and Athens
Paul at Ephesus
Paul Before Felix
Paying the Price for Souls
Persecution
Perseverance and Fruitfulness
Peter's Advice on Christian Living
Peter's Message on Pentecost
Satan's Servants
Self-Esteem and the Christian
Serious Christian Living
Some of the Most Important Truths that Were Ever Taught
Spiritual Nearsightedness
Suffering for the Name
Temptations and Sin's Effects
Tests that Come Our Way
The Antichrist and False Prophet
The Blood of Jesus Christ
The Certainty of Judgment Day
The Command, "Do Not Love"
The Cries of the Damned
The Enormous Red Dragon
The Fear of God
The Fear of Man
The Final Word on Who is Blessed
The Great From God's Perspective
The Greatest Questions Ever Asked
The Importance of Follow-Up
The Importance of Jesus' Resurrection
The Intensity of Our Warfare
The Judgment of Believers, I
The Judgment of Believers, II
The Name of Jesus
The One Who Sits on the Throne
The Peculiar Love of the Lord Jesus
The Preeminence of Truth
The Race Marked Out For Us
The Reliability of the Bible, I
The Reliability of the Bible, II
The Righteous Trio
The Roman Catholic Gospel
The Temporal versus the Eternal
The Three Views of the Rapture, I
The Three Views of the Rapture, II
The Trinity
The True Servant of God
The War Against Your Soul
The Why and How of Memorizing Scripture
Those That Go To Hell
Uzziah
What's Right and What's Wrong with The Present-Day Faith Message
Wisdom, More Precious Than Rubies
You Have Forgotten Your First Love

*Free with purchase of Bible Study Methods II and III.